THE MOVIE
MAKERS **BRANDO**

BRANDO

David Shipman

Doubleday & Co. Inc.

Garden City, New York, 1974

Front Endpaper: *The Appaloosa*

Back Endpaper: *The Nightcomers*

Half-title: *A Streetcar Named Desire*

Title page: *The Wild One*

© David Shipman 1974

ISBN 0-385-01045-1

Library of Congress Catalog Card Number 73-11635

Designed by Paul Watkins and Florianne Henfield

First Edition in the United States of America

First published 1974 by
Macmillan London Limited
London and Basingstoke
Associated companies in New York, Toronto,
Dublin, Melbourne, Johannesburg and Madras

Filmset in Plantin and
printed in Great Britain
by Jolly and Barber Ltd., Rugby
Bound by Dorstel Press Ltd., Harlow

Contents

For Jane and Gordon

Brando: no one who goes to see him, having seen him once before, could want him to do anything but succeed, be better than he was before. He inspires that sort of confidence and excitement. No one who has seen him act could be entirely indifferent to the sort of man he is off the screen. Since he first appeared on that screen, he has been, quite simply, the first actor of his generation.

1 THE BEGINNINGS

Brando aged 15 at the Shattuck Military Academy. A face with a fortune.

arlon Brando is his real name. His father was also a Marlon Brando – the name is an Anglicization of the French 'Brandeau'. Marlon Brando Sr married a Dorothy Pennebaker; Marlon Jr was born on April 3rd, 1924, the youngest of three children and the only boy. They were living then in Omaha, Nebraska, where Mrs Brando was a director of the local Community Playhouse. She was an enthusiastic amateur actress, and had acted with Henry Fonda – then living in Omaha – before he turned professional.

When Marlon Jr (nicknamed 'Bud') was six, the family moved to Evanstown, Illinois; they moved again, to California, and then returned to Illinois, to a town called Libertyville – a name which is appropriate in view of the fierce independence Brando has carried with him through life. The local high school called him 'irresponsible', and he was no scholar. His father removed him and sent him to his own old school, a military academy, the Shattuck Academy in Minnesota, from which he was expelled shortly before graduation. The United States had by this time entered the War, but Brando did not serve, being graded 4-F because of a trick knee. For six weeks he worked in the open, digging ditches; then he went to New York, to a series of elementary, almost-bumming jobs. He lived with his sister Frances, who was studying art. Brando Sr was a successful businessman, and he offered to finance Brando Jr for training in whatever trade or profession he cared to follow. He chose acting. He was nineteen.

His mother's influence had already pointed his other sister, Jocelyn, towards the theatre (she would later make a few films, including *The Big Heat*, playing Glenn Ford's wife, and supporting her brother in *The Ugly American* and *The Chase*), and he had done some dramatics at the military academy. He enrolled at the Dramatic Workshop of the New School for Social Research on 12th Street, and he studied there for a year under Erwin Piscator, the German expressionist director. For an outfit called The Children's Theater, the Dramatic Workshop put on a play at the Adelphi Theater in New York – 'Bobino', written for the occasion by Stanley Kauffman. Brando had two roles in what could be regarded as his professional debut; a giraffe and a guard. The following year – 1944 – Piscator invited him to join him for a stock season at the Sayville Summer Theater on Long Island. He did two plays before being fired: a once-famous German play, 'Hannele's Way to Heaven' (known in Britain as 'Hannele'), by Gerhart Hauptmann, in which he played another dual role, a teacher and an angel, and 'Twelfth Night', as Sebastian.

On the day he left he signed a contract, arranged by an agent who had seen him at Sayville. It was for a Broadway play, 'I Remember Mama', John Van Druten's dramatization of a memoir by Kathryn Forbes, concerned with a Norwegian –American family in San Francisco. Van Druten

Previous page:
Brando on his arrival in Hollywood

Left: Brando's Broadway debut: with Frances Heflin, Nancy Marquand, Oscar Homolka in *I Remember Mama* at the Music Box, 1944

9

directed, Mady Christians was Mama, and Brando was one of her children, the fifteen-year-old Nels. It opened at the Music Box in October to excellent notices, some of which singled Brando out for a line of praise; and it ran two years.

He continued to study. He moved on to Stella Adler, who taught acting according to the principles laid down by Stanislavsky. These, briefly stated, include complete realism, ensemble acting, and an absolute identification with the character – which can lead to complexities whereby the actor might delve into the character's subconscious, or move in his time-and-space process. The layman knows this as Method acting, or as 'the Method', and it has been much dissected and analysed since Brando became famous (and the two matters are not coincidental). The discussions, I suspect, were of little interest to the public, who had already discerned the fact that all good actors have a method. Laurence Olivier has said so; so has Bette Davis – and in passing we might note her comment (in her memoir) on the Method and Brando: 'They have simply learned to express themselves; and I'm terribly happy for them. When they learn to express the character, I shall applaud them.... Then there's the question of style. Without it, there is no art. As personal as these troubled actors are, there is – aside from much of a muchness – the same of a sameness. They are all so busy revealing their own insides that, like all X-ray plates, one looks pretty much like the other. Their godhead, the remarkably gifted Marlon Brando, may bring (as all true stars do) his own personal magnetism to every part, but his scope and projection are unarguable. He has always transcended the techniques he was taught. His consequent glamour and style have nothing to do with self-involvement but rather radiation.'

The Method – the one with the capital M – may be said to refer to the practitioners of the Stanislavsky rules, as adopted by some earnest theatre people in New York whose thoughts and theories on the subject were coming to fruition at the time Brando took up acting. The names of the teachers and trainers are as well known outside the profession as their features are cloudy: Miss Adler, Robert Lewis, Lee Strasberg, Herbert Berghof and Elia Kazan, among others. Strasberg and Kazan later founded the Actors' Studio, and Brando studied under them. With the Actors' Studio or with the other names would be associated almost every major American acting talent to emerge over the next generation. Discontented or ambitious Hollywood stars – like Marilyn Monroe and Shelley Winters – went to the Studio classes as 'observers'; Anne Bancroft studied there after her Broadway success in 'Two for the Seesaw'.

The renown and fame of the Studio – the fact that the general public heard of it – is directly attributable to Brando, often in connection with the 'mumbling' and 'scratching and

itching' which are supposed to have characterized his work –
and I am quoting from 'Actors Talk About Acting' by Lewis
Funke and John E. Booth, in questions about Brando put to
Morris Carnovsky and Maureen Stapleton. Both performers
refuted the suggestion that such gestures were typical of
Method acting; and on another occasion Miss Stapleton
observed that 'someone like Marlon Brando is so complete
a talent that he can draw on things inside himself for what
he needs. He has more equipment for doing this than most
people.'

It took Brando a long time to live down such accusations
(those interviews were published in 1961), and they were
directed at him because he was the most famous of the alumni
– though, of course, his first famous role was not exactly
brother to John (or is it Ernest?) Worthing. Kim Hunter, who
played with him then, later noted one of his major qualities:
'an uncanny sense of truth. It seems absolutely impossible for
him to be false. It makes him easier to act with than anybody
else ever. Anything you do that may not be true shows up
immediately as false with him.' One of the things he was doing
was pushing realism to the extreme.

The new realism could be said to have been demanded by
wartime and postwar audiences, no longer content to be lied
to; but realism had been with theatre audiences, long before it
was ever chanted by Stanislavsky. Nineteenth-century audiences had wanted to see realistic flames when the barn burned
down in the last act; old playbills boast of waterfalls and ava-
lanches. Popular successes like 'The Scarlet Pimpernel' and
'The Only Way' realistically re-created the Terror when their
actors donned the clothes of that era; it was the view of the
Universe which was romantic till the first chill notes were
struck by Ibsen. Later, a Galsworthy or so offered a 'social
conscience' play, but amidst so many melodramas and farces
realism lay like a slumbering dog. Its eventual awakening was
inevitable once the cinema took over the mass-marketing of
fairy-tales – for the cinema was obviously a realistic medium,
proffering not only Mary Pickford's curls and Chaplin's jaunty
walk but the revolutionaries of Pudovkin's *Mother* and the
peasants of Dovzhenko's *Earth* – and I cite Russian examples
because the new realism of the American theatre in the thirties
was distinctly left-wing, though the reason (if directly attributable at all) has probably less to do with the experiments in
Soviet Russia than the Depression. The most influential
theatre organization of the time, the Group Theater, was
founded in 1931 by a group of breakaways from the Theatre
Guild, the most prestigious and successful New York producer – to wit, Cheryl Crawford, Lee Strasberg and Harold
Clurman (who was married to Stella Adler at the time Brando
was her pupil). Luther Adler, Stella's brother, acted for the
Group; so did Carnovsky, Franchot Tone, Lee J. Cobb and

The Group Theatre. A scene from *Golden Boy*, produced in 1937. From left to right: Lee J. Cobb, Phoebe Brand, John Garfield, Luther Adler, Morris Carnovsky and Frances Farmer. The portrait is of Cheryl Crawford, co-founder of the Group. The company picture, taken c.1938, shows (back row) Art Smith, Walter Fried, Sanford Meisner, Ruth Nelson, Lee J. Cobb, Leif Ericson, Roman Bohnen, Morris Carnovsky, Kermit Bloomgarden, (front row) Luther Adler, Phoebe Brand, Harold Clurman, Eleanor Lynn, Frances Farmer, Robert Lewis, Elia Kazan and (seated on the floor) Irwin Shaw

John Garfield, all in their tyro days. Robert Lewis and Kazan were trained with the Group. They put on 'realistic' plays – by Irwin Shaw, Robert Ardrey, Sidney Kingsley and William Saroyan – and Clifford Odets, whose 'Waiting for Lefty' and 'Golden Boy' were the Group's biggest successes.

With time and fame, the Group broke up and dispersed: the reforming zeal of Odets evaporated, and without it his plays were mediocre. The individual talents found lucrative employment elsewhere. At the beginning of 1946, Clurman and Kazan teamed up with the Playwrights' Company (also a breakaway from the Theatre Guild) to present Maxwell Anderson's 'Truckline Cafe'. Clurman directed a cast headed by Virginia Gilmore, David Manners and Brando, and including Karl Malden and Kevin McCarthy. The play was of the same genre as 'The Time of Your Life' and 'Small Craft Warnings', only this time the inmates were contemplating the postwar world. Brando played a young ex-soldier, Sarge McRae, who murders his wife when he learns of her infidelity during his

absence. The notices were poor – Brooks Atkinson later called
it 'a maudlin, routine melodrama' – and the author took an
advertisement in *The New York Times* castigating the critics.
All the same, the play only lasted thirteen performances.

Brando's own notices were good, and as a result he was
approached by Katherine Cornell and Guthrie McClintic to
appear in one of her periodic revivals of 'Candida'. She of
course would be Candida; the husband (McClintic) would
direct; and Wesley Addy and Cedric Hardwicke had been cast
as Morell and Burgess respectively. Brando would play
Marchbanks, the young poet who worships the older Candida
(Shaw specifies thirty-three; Miss Cornell was forty-eight at
this time) and is confident that he can woo her from her parson
husband. The role was played in an earlier Cornell production
by the previous *wunderkind* of American show business, also
then in his pre-fame days, Orson Welles. The play opened in
April, and Brando's performance was, on the whole, well
received; but I have spoken to several people who saw it, and

they shudder at the memory: 'unfortunate' is one summing-up of the interpretation. Marchbanks is not easy to play, despite Shaw's clinical description: 'a strange, shy youth of eighteen, slight, effeminate, with a delicate childish voice, and a hunted tormented expression and shrinking manner that show the painful sensitiveness of very swift and acute apprehensiveness in youth. . . . Miserably irresolute, he does not know where to stand or what to do.'

Certainly by the time the play had completed its brief run, Brando was going lightly on neither 'the hunted tormented expression' nor the irresolution. Jim Henaghan, later the Hollywood columnist, knew Brando at this time and says that except in one respect, Marchbanks was the reverse of Brando as he then was. He was remarkably self-assured, Henaghan says, but he was certainly effeminate; the mannerisms thus implied disappeared when he went on stage in 'A Streetcar Named Desire' and, Henaghan adds, in life as well around the same time. He was always polite and friendly towards Henaghan; to other columnists he was rude, but he wasn't entirely unjustified, whichever reaction he took. He was, then as now, an enigma to casual acquaintances and journalists – and often to his friends. He shared an apartment with a fellow-actor, Wally Cox (a friendship which lasted till Cox's death), but was regarded as a loner. He might appear unexpectedly, and disappear as quietly as he came; sometimes it seemed he only materialized in order to eat all the food in the house or change his clothes (for those of the host; socks, mainly). That he had, beneath the bonhomie and practical joking, problems, was evident to Kazan, who sent him to his own analyst. Two words sum up Brando's private life: ambiguous and ambivalent. You might add, devious. The total sum of his interviews, his public statements and reported remarks are consistent only in being inconsistent; some people have found him blindingly intelligent, and others stupid; with some he has been co-operative, with others not. He has frequently said that he despises acting, but before returning to his career we might pause at a statement he made in 1960: 'An actor must interpret life, and in order to do so he must be willing to accept all experiences that life can offer. In fact, he must seek out more of life than life puts at his feet. In the short span of his life, an actor must learn all there is to know; experience all there is to experience; or approach that shape as closely as possible. He must be superhuman in his endless struggle to inform himself. He must be relentless in his efforts to store away in the warehouse of his subconscious everything he might be called upon to know and use in the expression of his art. Nothing should be more important to the artist than life and the living of it, not even the ego. To grasp the full significance of life is the actor's duty, to interpret it his problem, and to express it his dedication.'

2 BROADWAY FAME

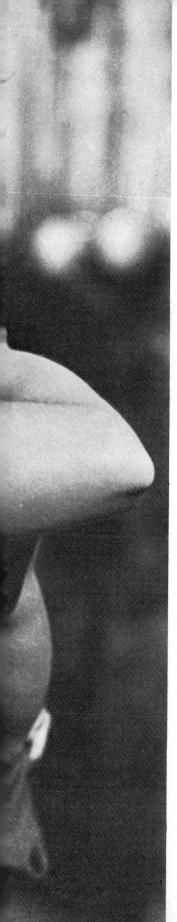

'Candida' ran till the end of the season. In September, Brando opened at the Alvin in a play sponsored by the American League for a Free Palestine, 'A Flag is Born', a pageant by Ben Hecht with music by Kurt Weill. The cast was headed by Paul Muni and Celia Adler; Brando had the third most important role, as David, an embittered Jewish boy. Luther Adler directed, and took on Muni's role when the play moved to the Music Box the following month. It did not run: like most good causes allied to art, neither was well-served, and ethnic interest was little stirred.

Brando was then engaged by John C. Wilson to play opposite Tallulah Bankhead in 'The Eagle Has Two Heads', Jean Cocteau's wish-fulfilment fantasy about a peasant assassin who comes to kill the Queen but stays to love her. Cocteau had written it for Edwige Feuillère and Jean Marais (both about to make the film version), and in England, in the same translation, by Ronald Duncan, it had just made Eileen Herlie a star. The play was not good, and by all accounts it was not Miss Bankhead's most shining hour; but that was no reason why, during her 20-minute-long First Act speech, Brando should have scratched, picked his nose, examined his fly, etc. The night Wilson saw his performance, in the Boston try-out, he also, after finally killing the Queen, was himself unconscionably long in dying, threshing about the stage till he found a suitable resting-place. He was replaced by Helmut Dantine, an Austrian-born Warner Bros second lead of the war years.

It was Kazan who suggested Brando for the role of Kowalski in 'A Streetcar Named Desire'. Tennessee Williams's writing, after a flop play ('Battle of Angels' in 1940) and a spell as an M-G-M scriptwriter, had found eloquent expression in a memory piece, 'The Glass Menagerie'. Returning to New Orleans, he resurrected from earlier one-act plays (many of his later three-act plays are reworkings of his early plays and stories) the character of a faded Southern belle on the edge of self-destruction, Blanche du Bois, who arrives in New Orleans to stay with her sister Stella and her husband, Stanley. Stanley Kowalski is, as the play says, a Polack, and even without Blanche's pretensions it is clear that Stella has married beneath her, and probably for what a later generation would call 'a good screw'. Kowalski is elemental; as Williams describes him: 'Animal joy in his being is implicit in all his movements and attitudes. Since early manhood the centre of his life has been pleasure with women . . . with the power and pride of a richly feathered male bird among hens. Branching out from this complete and satisfying centre are all the auxiliary channels of his life, such as his heartiness with men, his appreciation of rough humour, his love of good drink and food and games, his car, his radio, everything that is his, that bears his emblem of the gaudy seed-bearer. He sizes women up at a glance, with sexual classifications, crude images flashing into his mind and determining the way he smiles at them.'

In 1947 on Broadway there were plays about British justice ('The Winslow Boy'), a Henry James spinster ('The Heiress') and U.S.A.F. executives ('Command Decision'). It was unthinkable that anyone would want to write or present a play in which a man sizes up his sister-in-law sexually. At a cursory glance, 'Streetcar' is a study of sexual antagonism. The 'plain man', Stanley, rebels at Blanche's dreams and fantasies – of the now-gone family mansion – because they remind him too forcibly of his own inferiority ('I'm afraid I'll strike you as the unrefined type'); he resents her airs, so he's jubilant when he can expose her: 'That's why she's here this summer, visiting royalty, putting on all this act – because she's practically told by the mayor to get out of town! Yes, did you know there was an army camp near Laurel and your sister's was one of the places "Out-of-Bounds"?' He's equally intrigued: the cuckoo in the nest is a whore. In turn, Blanche criticizes him to Stella: 'He acts like an animal, has an animal's habits! Eats like one, moves like one, talks like one! ... Thousands and thousands of years have passed him right by, and there he is – Stanley Kowalski – survivor of the Stone age.' His discovery of her past, and her acknowledgement of his animalism lead to sexual congress: with Stella in hospital, he rapes Blanche, saying 'We've had this date with each other from the beginning'.

The line is, fortunately, not typical of the play. Although it scandalized New York and later London it was immediately realized that Williams had written a compassionate, poetic piece, rough-romantic, tough-tawdry, silken-sophisticated; and he had created two remarkable leading characters. Blanche and Kowalski offered one of the classic confrontations of twentieth-century drama: she is a lady, a butterfly, a hypocrite, 'a cultivated woman', as she puts it, 'a woman of intelligence and breeding'; he is a rough diamond, a slob, an honest Joe, the guy in the street. He will crush her.

Because he feared that the role of Blanche overshadowed Stanley, John Garfield turned it down. Burt Lancaster was offered it, he says, because of his performance in his first film, *The Killers*, but he had a film to do. Kazan sent Brando to see Williams, and in an interview in *Esquire* Williams spoke of their first meeting: 'He arrived at dusk, wearing Levi's, took one look at the confusion around him, and set to work. First he stuck his hand into the overflowing toilet and unclogged the drain, then he tackled the fuses. Within an hour, everything worked. ... Then he read the script aloud, just as he played it. It was the most magnificent reading I ever heard and he had the part immediately. He stayed the night, curled up with a quilt on the floor.'

Blanche was played by Jessica Tandy, the first of several British-born actresses to play the role. Kim Hunter played Stella and Karl Malden was Mitch, the card-playing crony of

Stanley's whom Blanche almost managed to marry. Kazan directed, and the play opened at the Ethel Barrymore on 3 December 1947, under the auspices of Irene M. Selznick (the estranged wife of David O. Selznick, and daughter of Louis B. Mayer). The play, the production and the performances were uniformally praised; it won both the Drama Critics Circle award as the best play of the year and the Pulitzer Prize; it was easily the hottest ticket in town, and went on to play 855 performances.

Miss Tandy left after six months to tour with the play, and was succeeded by Uta Hagen. Queried about the best of the Blanches in 1973 (when the play was revived on Broadway with Rosemary Harris and James Darren), Williams agreed that possibly Miss Hagen was the one, but he'd always felt 'closest' to Miss Tandy; he volunteered the information that no one had equalled Brando as Kowalski, and added that no one should try to imitate his performance.

Below: The film of *Streetcar* again: Blanche's birthday party—Brando, Vivien Leigh and Miss Hunter

3 INTO FILMS

Brando fretted during the run of the play. He had achieved the sort of acclaim which brought Hollywood offers, and none came. He was bored with the play, and consoled only by the fact that he was now a stage star, which meant, in practical terms, that the next time round he could command a higher salary than at present ($550 weekly) and have greater freedom in his choice. Although the publicity line, later, was than he turned down scores of offers, Jim Henaghan says that Brando begged him to get him a film contract, but no producer was interested.

Hollywood had at that time all the new faces it needed, for the public then was showing a marked preference for the old faces. The accredited male box-office stars in 1949 and 1950 were Bing Crosby, Bob Hope, Abbott and Costello, John Wayne, Gary Cooper, Cary Grant, Humphrey Bogart, Clark Gable, James Stewart, Spencer Tracy, Clifton Webb and Randolph Scott; hovering just below the top-listed ten in the *Motion Picture Herald*'s compilations were Tyrone Power, Errol Flynn, Alan Ladd, Robert Taylor and James Cagney. Leaving aside Abbott & Costello and Webb as special cases (they were 'funny-men'), Ladd was the only one who had been around less than ten years (i.e. as a star); most of the others went back fifteen years or more. The studios were, as ever, industriously finding vehicles for them, and if they wanted new blood, there was some around: some independent, none tied exclusively to one studio – Gregory Peck, Kirk Douglas, Burt Lancaster, Montgomery Clift. And if they were being offered more work than they could handle, there were lesser contract stars to be kept busy, like Glenn Ford and William Holden at that time.

The offer which Brando accepted was from an independent company which couldn't afford – and for this project certainly didn't want – a high-priced star name. The film was *The Men*, and it was the effort of a group of men – a felicitous coming-together of talents – considered the industry's new white hopes. Critics and what can succinctly be described as serious film buffs looked to these men to provide relief from the fantasies of the dream factory – to face film life more realistically and with maturity. They were Stanley Kramer, the producer, Carl Foreman, who wrote *The Men*, and Fred Zinnemann who was to direct it. They were all old Hollywood hands.

Kramer had begun in films in 1933 in the research department of M-G-M; he had been cutter and casting director, and in the early forties had assisted Albert Lewin on the production of *So Ends Our Night* and *The Moon and Sixpence*. Lewin was a producer who did not underestimate public taste (though the public often had little taste for the ambitious works he offered it); his philosophies seem to have rubbed off on Kramer, who, after a minor comedy in 1948, *So This is New York*, embarked on a series of resolutely non-escapist films.

The first, *Champion*, was a fierce and unsentimental study of a prize-fighter (Kirk Douglas); made on a modest budget and liked by both press and public, it made a lot of money. *Home of the Brave*, the second venture, was a version of a Broadway play about racial intolerance in the army: there was prestige but little profit. United Artists distributed both, and they would handle *The Men*, but for that Kramer had had to find a new backer. Foreman had co-scripted or adapted Kramer's productions up to now. He had been in Hollywood since at least 1941, when he received a credit as one of the writers of *Spooks Run Wild*; after working on such ignoble projects as *Bowery Blitzkreig*, *Rhythm Parade* and *Dakota*, he finally managed, with Kramer, to make the sort of films he wanted to make.

The only one of the three of any real accomplishment was Zinnemann. Born in Vienna, he worked in Germany on *Menschen am Sonntag*, in 1930, before reaching Hollywood. In 1937 he started work at M-G-M on their 'Crime Does Not Pay' series; he had moved over to features – B pictures – in 1941. In 1944 he directed Spencer Tracy in *The Seventh Cross*, one of the best of all anti-Nazi pictures (it concerned an anti-fascist on the run in the prewar Reich), and made his reputation with *The Search*, in 1948, a film about displaced children in postwar Europe.

Foreman wrote both story and screenplay of *The Men*, a study of paraplegics. There were about 2,500 paraplegics in the U.S. at this time, relics of the War, men permanently maimed – in dictionary terms, the lower half of their body paralysed on both sides. Foreman and Kramer talked to and studied many of them at the Birmingham Veterans Administration Hospital near Los Angeles, and it was there, later, that much of the piece was filmed. Zinnemann used several of the men in small roles, and Brando insisted on living in the hospital before filming began. There was also considerable rehearsal before the cameras were set up, which was unusual in Hollywood; but all concerned felt that the subject would benefit from a greater knowledge of the interplay of characters – and the result was a taut, tight film, with, paradoxically, a documentary-like spontaneity. The film was edgy, rough, and, by implication, deeply pacifist. Under the credits, soldiers advanced to the martial cry of drums; with a burst of machine-gun fire, the screen dissolves to the men in hospital.

One of them, an ex-officer, Ken Wilozek (Brando), alternates between gloomy silences and outbursts of self-mockery. He refuses to see his fiancée, Ellen (Teresa Wright), anxious to help him, because he feels that she is acting from pity; he greets the doctors with sullen sarcasm and is as prickly as a hedgehog when confronted with the kindness of fellow patients. They, like he, resort to irony, and he gradually emerges from isolation to mingle his bitterness with theirs. He also succumbs to therapy and training, and is finally encouraged to see Ellen. Her optimism falters when faced with a lifetime of coping with an invalid. His doctor (Everett Sloane) can offer no reassurances and her family opposes the marriage; and on the wedding night they quarrel.

In *Sight & Sound*, Richard Winnington conveyed the achievement of that sequence: 'The scene in which two persons who love each other deeply pour out the fruit of all their torment in irrational words of hate, is a hallmark of the truth of the film. It is one of the few love passages of the cinema to encompass the pitiful ache of human love.'

Ken returns to hospital, afraid; but on the pretext of a drunken spree the governors of the hospital expel him, believing that if he can make his marriage work there is no greater therapy. The film ends inconclusively, but on a note of hope.

It is conventional to say that a film like this must be moving: it is about sad matters, therefore it must be sad. It is inconceivable that it isn't so, but it is inconceivable without the tact, the passion and the honesty of the handling here. Zinnemann's ability to get it down plain even papers over some of the faults, seemingly indigenous at the time, to the 'social problem' picture. A difficult subject requires an exceptional talent, and he had it. Stanley Kramer, later, when he turned director, would be inadequate to almost every subject he handled; but there is no doubt that in 1950, he, Foreman and Zinnemann made a film better (i.e. better-made, more involving, with more substance) than any other American film that year.

The reviews were entirely laudatory, and Brando's ability was at once acknowledged. Winnington said that 'his combination of style, depth and range comes like a blood transfusion into cinema acting' and Otis L. Guernsey, in the *New York Herald-Tribune*, noted that the performance 'depends not at all on personality but entirely on understanding of character and technical virtuosity'. We were not accustomed to this in Hollywood pictures. Spencer Tracy, regarded by many as the best living screen actor at that time, delved deeper into himself instead of casting wider (and when asked why he always played himself, growled, 'Who do you expect me to play – Humphrey Bogart?'). We enjoyed the virtuosity of Bogart and Cagney, without kidding ourselves that they played other than variations of themselves. Only occasionally did a star actor maintain his position by exploiting versatility: Charles Laughton was one, and he had to, because he was not by nature a leading man; Paul Muni was another, and it was only after a while that

it was realized that under the various beards there was the same performance going on. Unless you're content to play yourself, the use of make-up is a legitimate device: Laughton and Muni tried never to look alike twice – a theory to which Laurence Olivier, on stage and screen, was the most notable adherent. Brando would follow them, but would use less artificial aids.

His achievement at this stage, in *The Men*, was to offer a complete study instead of the bits of himself a movie-star offers to the saying of the dialogue. We sensed rather than knew that it was a character performance: men under stress and neurotics are not unusual in movies, but even with natural-sounding dialogue there was something we hadn't experienced before. Ken Wilozek was outwardly tortured and inwardly twisted – the sort of terms in which such heroes could be summarized – but there was an unexpected sense of ordinariness: this was a young man who had never expected to amount to very much, he'd never expected he'd have to think deeply or read the right books, much less question the fate which had dealt him this blow, setting him apart from his fellows. It was clear that Brando himself was not at all ordinary.

Brando and Teresa Wright in a publicity shot issued in conjunction with *The Men*

4 TWO BY KAZAN

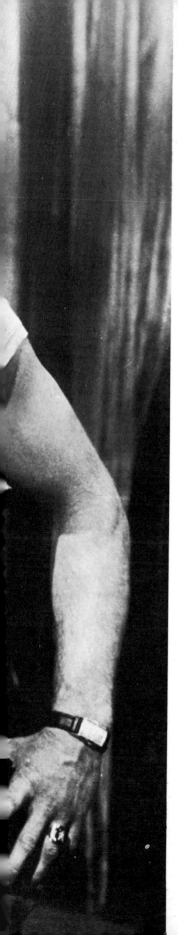

he Men opened in New York at Radio City Music Hall, but its reception by the public reflected only the optimism of its backers. Kramer's avowed policy was to offer the best possible films on limited budgets, using inexpensive but appropriate talents (Brando's fee was $50,000, about one-third of what the big stars commanded per film). *The Men* appeared on several lists of the year's best films, but to the New York critics that year the best possible film was *All About Eve*. The public liked *Samson and Delilah*, Disney's *Cinderella*, *King Solomon's Mines*, *Battleground* and *Annie Get Your Gun*. The time had not yet come when queues formed at the instigation of critics.

But if Brando was praised in the reviews, the feature pages presented him as a surly young man who went about in T-shirts and blue jeans and was rude to Louella Parsons. Co-operative and conscientious on set, he was equally painstaking in showing contempt for Hollywood people. Sifting through all the stuff written about the young Brando, the 'rebel', I think it is clear that he set out to outrage or antagonize the self-important denizens of tinsel-town, but, like his rejection of the Oscar twenty-three years later, he seems to have taken them at their own importance. His antics read foolishly because you wish he'd been big enough to ignore the Heddas and Louellas and the cigar-chomping tin gods. The press has always trivialized colourful or independent minds working in show business: it's a shame, it is inconvenient, like a hangover. Brando never seems to have adjusted.

There had been, before, other actors – usually from Broadway – who refused to play the Hollywood game. Katharine Hepburn was one, and George Cukor later observed that it wasn't she who had grown up to Hollywood but vice versa. Hollywood would learn to love Brando, as it always loves success, but whenever it folded him to its bosom over the years, he struck back like a spoilt child. He chose that pool to paddle in: but whoever thought that actors should lay claim to diplomacy?

It was still uncertain at this point whether he could command a real star's fee or a real star's power; because movies so seldom accommodated an actor of this sort, it was widely thought that he would return to the stage – to eventually tackle the classics. He did a television play in 1950 – 'Come Out Fighting' for N.B.C., in which he played a prize-fighter – but has evinced no subsequent interest in that medium (he has been interviewed on TV, but less than ten times in twenty years – less than some promoters do in a week). After *The Men*, he didn't lack film offers. At R.K.O., Wald and Krasna announced *The Harder They Fall*, saying that they had in mind Brando, Kirk Douglas or John Garfield as the pugilist (it wasn't made till six years later). Brando was often bracketed with Douglas as the new 'strong' actor.

Previous pages:
A Streetcar Named Desire:
the pose that launched a
thousand T-shirts

His next film role was the expected one – in the film of 'A Streetcar Named Desire'. The rights had been purchased by an agent, Charles K. Feldman, who had motion picture aspirations. In 1944, for Universal, he had produced *Follow the Boys*, an all-star jollity containing many of his clients. He returned to films in 1950, co-producing with Warner Bros the film of Tennesee Williams's 'The Glass Menagerie'; he arranged another deal with Warners for *Streetcar*, signing Kazan to direct, Brando to play Kowalski (at a fee of $75,000), and Vivien Leigh to re-enact the Blanche she had done in the London production.

The film was not a cast-iron proposition. The play had been praised, but there weren't many laughs, and it was doubtful whether the film public would support a subject which ends with its heroine being led off to a mental institution. The ad-copy could emphasize the 'sizzling! scorching!' aspects, but though the Hays Office had passed the screenplay (with the exception of a tacit reference by Blanche to her husband's homosexuality), some local authorities might object. In the event, the film was so well-received by the press as to ensure an easy journey; whether attracted or not by a degree of scandal, the public turned up in huge numbers.

Kazan had not wanted to make it; he felt that he had finished with it years before, but took on the job because Williams urged him to. They worked out a screenplay, opening it out, but at the last minute went back to the original play and filmed that. It remains the most persuasive of photographed plays. It starts with a cliché: Blanche appears out of a puff of smoke, like Garbo in *Anna Karenina* – but it was probably done in emulation. There is a fake poetry in the early reaches of the film, a combination of peeling stucco, Ufa lighting, Alex North's heartbreak-jazz score; but it is entirely suitable to what Blanche is saying or dreaming. She is a larger-than-life figure (Williams created her so; and Kazan has said that he had difficulty in getting Miss Leigh to abandon her stereotyped and theatrical conception of the role), dumped into a New Orleans of recognizably proletarian taste, but not of much realism. The effect is, intentionally or not, extraordinarily like the stylized Berlin of *The Last Laugh*, in which, in a different way, Jannings was as bizarre as Blanche; his dismissal is as effective as her expulsion from grace, in that with the shock they are both in an unreal, alien world. Kazan, in fact, found a texture to accommodate the text – and into it Brando slotted with ease.

Kowalski is perhaps one of Blanche's fantasies – the most substantial of them. Against her extravagances his excesses, even his bellowing and grunting, pale. Despite the title (Desire is a district of New Orleans), their mutual appraisal is dependent on selfishness rather than lust. Her posturing is somewhat antiseptic – at least the way Vivien Leigh plays her

(I've seen no other actress do it, and can't imagine another): it has rather to do with the hope that Stanley, or *someone*, will recognize her gentility. She has been a coquette too long to be very sanguine, however, that she can go on holding off advances – and of course she doesn't want to: nymphomania is primarily selfish. He is more obviously motivated by sexual gratification, but he's concerned with the quality of his orgasm, not with hers – and she's fully aware of that.

Another set of actors, another director might not find these inferences in the text. With Miss Hunter and Karl Malden repeating from Broadway, this is the definitive *Streetcar*. Brando's performance encompassed everything that Williams had imagined into the character and set down in the text; and his presence made both silences and shouting awesome. One recognized, more than in *The Men*, that he generated the same sort of electricity as James Cagney: you felt that nothing either of them did was without danger, without tension. Brando was less volatile, and probably a better actor. As Kowalski, it was as if a spring uncoiled, and he became the most discussed actor in the world.

He was later to say that *Streetcar* was the only one of his films he liked. Then, it was cheered at the Venice Film Festival. The New York Critics Circle chose it the best film of the year – and Kazan as the best director. At the Academy Award ceremony, Oscars went to Miss Leigh, Miss Hunter and Mr Malden. Brando, of course nominated, lost to Humphrey Bogart in *The African Queen*, which could have meant that the Academy wanted to slap him down or even that its members loathed Kowalski as much as Brando had said he did. More likely, Bogart won from a combination of Academy sentiment and his own merit. Also, Hollywood people are sometimes realists (in things which concern Hollywood), and it was clear that Brando would be heard from much in the future. His third picture had been shown before the Academy ballots went out, and if things went on this way, the three feathers in his cap would be an Indian head-dress.

The film was *Viva Zapata!*, and Brando played the Mexican revolutionary leader, at the insistence of Kazan, again directing. Kazan credits himself with the inception of the film, in a conversation with John Steinbeck, who wrote it (though Howard Hawks once told *Cahiers du Cinema* that he had turned down the project). Steinbeck's source, uncredited on the screen, was a novel by Edgcumb Pinchon, 'Zapata the Unconquerable', which M-G-M had bought in 1940 as a vehicle for Robert Taylor (M-G-M had some years earlier had a big success with *Viva Villa!*). In 1949, it was sold to 20th Century-Fox, who already owned a property about Zapata called 'The Beloved Rogue'. It was perhaps because of this that Kazan and Steinbeck went to Darryl F. Zanuck at Fox. Zanuck had earlier produced the movie of Steinbeck's 'The Grapes of

Wrath', and he decided to take producer credit on this: they hoped for something equally prestigious. Steinbeck was fully aware of the danger to his reputation if he tampered with history to produce the usual Hollywood concoction, but, with Kazan's co-operation, tamper he did. The result is still a challenging piece on great matters, unequivocally the best movie – there are few competitors – on revolt between Eisenstein in the twenties and *La Battaglia di Algeri*.

As the film has it, Zapata is a Mexican Indian, well-born but penniless. In 1909 he was one of a party from a remote province, Morelos, come to Mexico City to complain that their arable land has been enclosed, leaving them only the barren hills; his expressed dissatisfaction with the response of the president, Diaz, puts him in danger, and when he rashly rescues a prisoner from the local militia he becomes an outlaw. Urged on by a strolling intellectual, Fernando (Joseph Wiseman), he supports the exiled Madero against Diaz, and becomes the leader of his forces in the South as Pancho Villa is in the North. Diaz flees, and Madero takes his place; but he is a puppet president, in the hands of the leader of the army, Huerta, who has him assassinated when he tries to express solidarity for the men who fought for him. Zapata and Villa return to arms, and, successful in victory, seek to find a leader for the country. Unwillingly, Zapata takes the job, but, a while later, he responds to some petitioners from his own village with no more reassurance than had Diaz years before: realizing that with power his idealism has gone, he returns with them to Morelos – specifically to investigate their complaints against his brother (Anthony Quinn). New leaders take his place, and, egged on by the always surviving Fernando, they decide Zapata is a threat to their regime. He is trapped and shot.

The real Zapata remains an enigma. His creed was 'Tierra y Libertad', and his cause was land for the Indians; he remains a hero in Mexico because, unlike other dissidents, he took nothing for himself. His integrity was unquestioned, though, in the accepted manner of brigands, he murdered indiscriminately and pillaged – matters on which the film is mute. His twenty-six bigamous marriages have become one wooing and wedding to a miscast Jean Peters, but the most serious distortion concerns his relinquishment of the presidency, which was far more complex than a desire to return to decency (and, in fact, after Villa and Zapata had succeeded in overthrowing despotism, they maintained a joint – if uneasy – control for eight years, not the few months the film suggests for Zapata's presidency).

However, if the film takes liberties, chances and sometimes leave of its senses, it also manages a vivid picture of a country at war with itself, of an uneducated and listless peasantry, of an opportunistic and vicious militia; it suggests both the highs and lows of a revolutionary's life – and it does it with incisiveness (Kazan says that he learnt from *Paisa* 'to jump from crag to crag, rather than going all along the valleys'). There are several things which no longer work (the parallels between the two petitions, the symbolic use of Zapata's horse in the final shot) and the pseudo-poetic dialogue was never admirable. Both the photography and the score help to patch together the disparate elements – palace intrigues, violent fighting and the placid, almost-asleep life of the villages.

Brando's intensity provides what is then needed. His make-up establishes the image of the photographs; for the rest, he is sunk in contemplation till conscience beckons him into obstinacy or fury. As with Kowalski – and some later performances – he makes much of the man's inability to communicate or think deeply (this Zapata is obsessed by the fact that he can't read, by his lack of education – and it might be worth noting that some of Brando's comments on his own success refer back to the fact that he was a school drop-out). He sometimes gives the impression of being a small, lost boy, but he's simply different from those actors (Cooper, Gable, Tracy) who normally play leaders; never one to play the accepted way, he doesn't so cheerfully accept the burden. He refuses the leadership at one point, claiming 'I don't want to be the conscience of the world, I don't want to be the conscience of anybody', and with any other actor it would have been self-assertion; Brando is too honest to play it except with a lingering note of regret. It was the first time in films he played a man of destiny, a role to which he would return again and again; and, of course, the role comprehended the other side of his screen persona, the inarticulate, uneducated underdog. Whether he could have played the real Zapata remains unknown, but he could play Steinbeck–Kazan's Zapata; Zapata the idealist. The film was made because they wanted to express the ineffectiveness of idealistic revolutionaries (and also, perhaps, to justify Kazan's co-operation with the Senate Committee on Un-American Activities – an action deeply resented by former left-wing associates). Kazan has said: 'I believe in democracy. I believe that democracy progresses through internecine war, through constant tension – we grow only through conflict. And that's what a democracy is. In that sense, people have to be vigilant, and the vigilance is effective. I truly believe that all power corrupts. . . .' Kazan's explanation of the reasons behind *Zapata*'s philosophy can, in fact, be applied to virtually every 'political' film made in Hollywood, so we need not suppose that he discussed them with Brando. The same beliefs can certainly be found in virtually every film, later, over which Brando had power (as well, of course, in the next, a version of Shakespeare's 'Julius Caesar'); and if you look at most of them carefully, you might well suspect a hankering to play Zapata again and again.

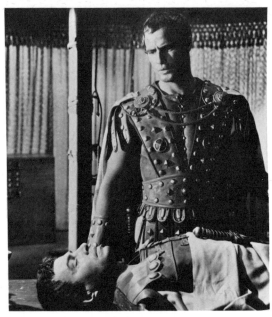

5 SCREEN STARDOM
AND SCREEN SHAKESPEARE

The excellent reviews for *Zapata* and its star (and he was judged the best actor for it at the Cannes Film Festival that year) cemented his position as the most solicited actor in town, or, in industry terms, the hottest property. After *The Men*, interest had been considerable; now, it was engulfing. Brando hesitated. *The Men* had opened in July 1950, *Streetcar* in September 1951, *Zapata* in February 1952; supremely confidant of his ability to floor Hollywood, he turned down long-term contracts with all the major studios, and wasn't concerned whether he went another year between films. His discernment (and he made six films before he blundered) only increased the admiration radiated in his direction.

He cast his eyes towards Europe, and flirted with a Zavattini script, *Stazione Termini*, with Autant-Lara directing, and which at one time Gérard Philipe had actually started. Ingrid Bergman was supposed to be the co-star of either actor, but then Selznick bought the property for Jennifer Jones (who made it with Montgomery Clift). Fred Zinnemann offered Brando a life of Van Gogh, and something called *The Red and the Blue*; Warner Bros hopefully announced *Black Ivory*, a pirate story which would reunite him with Vivien Leigh. Hardly less likely was an immersion in screen Shakespeare.

After three disastrous expeditions into Shakespeare in the early Talkie period, Hollywood had left the Bard well alone and/or to Laurence Olivier in Britain. However, at M-G-M, John Houseman, a more enterprising and more cultured producer than customary (he had been Orson Welles's partner at the Mercury Theater), had persuaded the Front Office that he could do a *Julius Caesar* for little cost (there were lots of togas left over from *Quo Vadis?* and they had only to be shipped from Rome) and much expectation of prestige. There would be several weeks' rehearsal, and the director would be an adroit handler of dialogue – Joseph L. Mankiewicz, returning to M-G-M for the first time since his days there as a producer. The cast would be paid, for the privilege of being part of the venture, less than they could normally command – John Gielgud (making his first American film, and his first film for more than a decade) as Cassius, James Mason as Brutus and Edmond O'Brien as Casca; plus three of Metro's contract players – Louis Calhern as Caesar, Greer Garson as Calpurnia and Deborah Kerr as Portia (the two ladies being in, clearly, for box-office purposes). M-G-M's choice for Mark Antony originally lay between Charlton Heston (who had played the role in a 16mm version, before his Hollywood career) and Leo Genn (who had impressed them in *Quo Vadis?*). But Houseman plumped for Brando, and he explained his reasons in *Theatre Arts Monthly*: '. . . there is no question in my mind that in natural equipment, temperament and application, he is one of the very great actors of our time'.

Left: *Julius Caesar*: Brando as Mark Antony haranguing the crowd and looking upon the body of Brutus (James Mason).
Below: The cast during rehearsals: from left to right: Louis Calhern, James Mason, John Gielgud, Greer Garson, Joseph L. Mankiewicz, Edmond O'Brien, Brando and Deborah Kerr

M-G-M happily used a still of one of the very great actors of our time stripped to the waist, to advertize the film, plus a simple but not-telling slogan, 'Greater than *Ivanhoe!*' In fact, the reviews sold it. It was an austere but straightforward account of the play, strong where it is strong, and faltering where the play is weak. The original has an unsatisfactory construction: it builds to the assassination of Caesar and Mark Antony's subsequent oration, then wanders into the matters of the rival factions which resulted, and their battles. In the film, the battle scenes were scrappily done, and it further suffers because it's a toss-up as to which actor will predominate; the later reaches of the play always seem to be searching for a tragic hero. It should be Brutus – but James Mason doesn't make it. He is up to the role, and his reading of it is intelligent, but his nobility is self-conscious, as if assumed for the film. By sheer skill, John Gielgud should make it; his Cassius is perfectly judged, and he wields the verse as a champion swordsman his weapon – but not even a study of this quality can hold Cassius to an audience. In his company, Brando is an amateur, and that is why, for all its qualities, his Mark Antony doesn't make it.

It is an astonishing performance (and it was more so then, when we didn't know his range), wrought with authority and a fierce controlled passion. It is by all means a success; the verse is well-spoken and without doubt to its meaning. But a vowel does get swallowed now and then, and Brando is neither suave enough nor elegant – a Roman general, perhaps, but a Roman statesman never. He is not dwarfed, and the film has almost the unity of Olivier's Shakespeare films. The play is very much the thing: you're never less than aware of Shakespeare's musings on the dangers of dictatorships, and of the mechanics to bring about their end, but in the end, the film is less a film than a record of some performances.

Mankiewicz, the director, offers an insight into Brando's methods: 'Marlon plunges into acting the way a deep-sea diver goes overboard. He keeps his eyes shut for hours to see what it's like to be without sight – in case he ever had to play a blind man. He practises using only his left hand for days so he'll know what it's like to play the part of a character who's lost his right hand.' And Olivier offers a comment on Brando's Mark Antony when asked about his imitators: 'I thought, god, that's me, it's so awful, is that all I've given to the world?' (He was referring specifically to Brando's rendering of 'Here was a Caesar! Whence comes such another?' His other comments on Brando, on N.B.C.'s 'Today Show', are revealing. Asked which actors he admired, he said 'Well, there's the obvious one: I adore Marlon Brando.' Pressed, he said they had something in common: 'Something, I can't describe it . . . the same channel of message, somehow, I think. He is a marvellous actor. I wouldn't compare myself to him.' Asked about Brando and the Actors' Studio technique – to 'get themselves into the part and it's inside out', he replied, 'Don't believe Marlon. Don't tell me he searches inside himself for everything. He looks out, too. He's peripheral, just as any other character actor is peripheral.')

Julius Caesar was premiered in New York in June 1953: it proved that Shakespeare on the screen was not Olivier's sole prerogative, and it did respectable business. Between the end of shooting and the opening, Brando had been to France and back. A French producer, Paul Graetz, had offered him the role of Sorel in a film version of Stendhal's 'Le Rouge et le Noir', and he had accepted. A few days before the agreed start, Brando changed his mind because, it was understood, he couldn't agree with the director, Claude Autant-Lara. Graetz sued for $150,000 – presumably the salary paid to Brando – and a few months later began the film with Gérard Philipe.

He turned down the remake of a French film, *Human Desire* (it had been *La Bete Humaine*), which Fritz Lang directed with Glenn Ford; he turned down the remake of *A Star is Born*, which James Mason eventually did. He was offered an independent *Sodom and Gomorrah*, and he may have turned down *Prince of Players*, a life of Edwin Booth which 20th Century-Fox announced as a vehicle for either him or Olivier (Richard Burton later played it). Because of the success of *Julius Caesar* there was a move at M-G-M to do either an *Antony and Cleopatra* with Brando and Ava Gardner, or a *Romeo and Juliet* with him and Pier Angeli: the latter, more probable project was abandoned when the Rank Organisation announced a British version to be directed by Renato Castellani. He was committed to *Pal Joey* at Columbia, with Billy Wilder directing him and Mae West, but the negotiations were tricky and the project abandoned (some years later, Frank Sinatra played it). In the summer of 1953 he did a summer stock tour in the Northeastern States, of Shaw's 'Arms and the Man', playing Sergius, the cynical, vain and rather ridiculous officer who loses the heroine to Bluntschi, the plain man, 'the chocolate soldier'. Bluntschi was played by William Redfield, who noted later – in 'Letters from an Actor' – that Brando's performance varied from day to day, from town to town.

It was his last stage performance. His subsequent lack of interest in the theatre probably justified this summing up later by Harold Clurman: 'Brando has developed an extraordinary series of rationalizations to justify his actions. One, he does what he does for money. Two, acting is neurotic, anyway. Three, movies are so powerful that by staying in them he is helping the world. What he is now, is a very good actor in movies. He is talented and intuitive, has a fine sense of language, but he is not a truly great actor. On Broadway, we tend to think of him as a useless good actor – that is, one with no real interest in acting for the sake of acting, nor in acting as a social force.'

6 TWO UNDERDOGS AND AN OSCAR

In the summer of that year, Brando also made a film, and his expressed disappointment in the result suggests that he was interested 'in acting as a social force'. It was *The Wild One*, produced by Stanley Kramer, directed by Laslo Benedek, who had worked for Kramer on *Death of a Salesman* (Zinnemann had been Kramer's first choice), and the film which established the image of Brando the rebel (in the sixties, when the poster craze came in, the posters of the now-podgy actor were always from *The Wild One*). Actually, in the film, read properly, Brando was less a rebel than a mixed-up kid – the sort one hoped annihilated later by 'Gee, Officer Krupke' in 'West Side Story'.

Brando's disenchantment with the finished film arose from the fact that 'instead of finding out why young people tend to bunch into groups that seek expression in violence, all we did was show the violence'. Yes, but till that time movies had offered only a stereotyped and dishonest view of violence; what was so startling here was the *gradual* way these thugs take over a town. John Paxton's screenplay is based on fact, and the original title – *The Cyclists' Raid* – is more accurate than the nebulously romantic one finally pinned on it. The British version (at least) starts with a foreword, 'This is a shocking story . . . ', which exhorts us all to see that it doesn't happen again; Brando's voice cuts in, telling how this town and a girl changed his life – and that's certainly a softening-up.

The motor-cyclists – the Blind Rebels Motorcycle Club – arrive in a small mid-Western town for some track races. The police move them on, and they stop for petrol in the next town. With their caps and leather jackets they're sinister in a quasi-military way, but the townspeople are friendly, even after a slight accident with an old man in a car: a brief altercation, an accusation of hooliganism, and one of the gang has to have his leg set in plaster. The gang hang around the local bar, and Johnnie, the leader (Brando), gets into conversation with the waitress, Kathie (Mary Murphy). Her dad (Robert Keith) is the town cop, and he doesn't want no trouble nohow.

They're about to blow when another gang arrives, led by Chino (Lee Marvin), an old buddy. Johnnie and Chino engage in a ritual trial of strength, watched by townsfolk only too pleased by something to break the monotony of their lives; but Chino cheeks the cop and is hauled off to jail. So his gang has a reason for staying; there's nothing to do but drink and sit around – but that's probably as much to do as there was back home. 'You don't have to go anywhere special' Johnnie tells the girl, 'that's cornball. You just go.' They're not violent, but they're bored; they play futile games on their bikes, and above all, they drink. Tension starts when they rough-house the beauty salon of the local flirts, and when they go to the jail intent on freeing Chino. Things are hotting up in the bar, and a group of the townsfolk are banding together.

Left: *The Wild One:* a posed still of Brando and the girl, Yvonne Doughty

And the gangs have terrorized Kathie: Johnnie rescues her like Prince Charming – and the film begins to fall apart. They stand upon a grassy knoll, and she calls upon him to explain himself. 'You think you're too good for me' he says, 'Anyone who thinks they're too good for me, I knock them down sometime.' We'd never had any doubts that Johnnie's trouble was insecurity, a pocket-Napoleon who talks of 'my boys' protectively. When the salon blonde learns the club's name, she asks: 'What're you rebelling against, Johnnie?' 'What've ya got?' is the quick reply; he has no other reply because he can't define boredom or middle-class stuffiness. He has little sense and less sensibility, and though his conversation with Kathie deviates from the hitherto realistic mood to Hollywood theorizing, Brando ensures that Johnnie remains inarticulate.

Back in town the townsmen grab him; his bike goes careering on, and a man is killed, an innocent spectator. 'Finally killed a man, eh?' says someone, a trite – if quick – way of saying that we're all responsible. The County Sheriff (Jay C. Flippen) arrives, and once the truth is told Johnnie is let off with an avuncular caution – and a rejoinder never to set foot in the town again. Before leaving (and in view of the level to which the film has sunk, we're not surprised) he goes to the bar to see the girl again.

She is weakly played, and given so many 'concern' close-ups that the film suffers. The rest of the cast is fine, and Brando is magnificent: cocky at the beginning among his own kind, he has the unsureness of adolescence among the adults at the end of the film. His long silences suggest a dumb brain trying to get its mechanism going, the mouth is weak, and the eyes shift, mirroring the master-boy mind behind. Physically, there are the itty-bitty side-burns, and the way he grooves to the juke-box: because of such things, twenty years later, after a run of officers and martyred heroes, he never would be thought of as a square actor.

In his next film he emerged again from the under-belly of society, in a performance so different as to be amazing. Brando's predecessor, the last actor to play rebels and chip-on-the-shoulder guys, was said by numerous commentators to be John Garfield; but once you've acknowledged Garfield's vitality, and a few minor changes of characterization, you're faced with an absolutely conventional performance, part sour-weary, part chin-up-and-take-it. Brando not only offered several new ways of looking at under-privileged heroes, but he played them as capable of varying moods and multitudinous thoughts and changes – all aspects of the man all at once. His performance in *On the Waterfront* is one of the most remarkable ever recorded on film.

Because of it, the film is the most famous, and it was the most successful, of all the 'social protest' films which Brando made; it was unanimously well-received, it broke box-office

Guys and Dolls:
Sky Masterson (Brando)
charming the church
Army Brigade. Jean
Simmons left, Regis
Toomey and two extras

records and it won a goodly number of awards. Kazan again directed, and it had been his idea to make a film about corruption on the docks. Budd Schulberg wrote the story and screenplay, from a series of articles by Malcolm Johnson, and Sam Spiegel produced for Columbia Pictures. Brando's role in particular is beautifully written: if it's his performance which sets this film above other films, he was well-helped.

He is Terry Malloy, ex-pug, longshoreman, close enough to the Mob because his brother, Charley the Gent (Rod Steiger), is the right-hand-man of Joe Friendly (Lee J. Cobb), who controls the docks. Any docker who doesn't toe the line is harassed, bullied – or killed. As one of them puts it, 'You don't ask questions and you don't answer questions on the docks'. The death of one man brings about the Crime Commissioners (Lief Erickson and Martin Balsam), and it spurs the anti-corruption crusade led by a fanatical local priest, Father Barry (Karl Malden).

Terry starts seeing the dead man's sister, Edie (Eva Marie Saint). 'Which side you on?' she asks. 'I'm with me' he replies. Later, 'You wanna hear my philosophy of life?' he asks, 'Do it to him before he does it to you. . . .Father Barry? What's his racket? Everyone's got a racket. . . . Down here it's every man for himself.' When a second man, another 'canary', is 'accidentally' killed, Terry is persuaded by the priest to confess to Edie his role in her brother's murder: 'It started out as a favour, who am I kidding? It was "do it or else". I thought they were just going to lean on him.' Because his is seen with the girl and the priest, Charley is sent to secure his brother's loyalty – but Terry has been compromised before: years before, they'd made him pull a fight at the Garden, and 'What did I get? – a one-way ticket to Palookaville. I coulda had class. I coulda been a contender.' Because of this, Charley doesn't warn him in the commanded fashion, and winds up dead.

As a result, Terry testifies to the Commission, and dockland turns against him; ignoring the contempt in which he's held, he turns up for work, and, when he isn't offered any, he takes on Friendly and the gang. Because he survives the beating-up, the men at last rally to him. It is his martyrdom and his atonement, and as the film works best as a study of awakening conscience, it is an effective climax.

The film also works as a thriller, organically constructed, but if it is not otherwise as seriously flawed as *The Wild One*, it does fall into almost every trap lying in wait for producers and directors of reforming zeal. It is brutally dishonest; it is over-composed and over-hysterical, with too much of the action in for electrifying effect. You might wonder why, at the end, the men are so slow to support Terry when Friendly and his gang expect imminent arrest: well, public ostracism is one thing, but even more blatant is the scene where Terry's teenage chum turns on him, having killed all his pigeons, 'A pigeon for a

Previous pages: *The Teahouse of the August Moon*. The large picture is a posed still of Brando, Machiko Kyo, Glenn Ford and one of the villagers. The smaller pictures show Brando as Sakini, wheedling and wangling, watched by an amused Glenn Ford

Overleaf: above, *The Wild One*. Brando on trial. Below, *On the Waterfront*: still Brando's most famous performance, and perhaps his most impressive. The girl is Eva Marie Saint who, like him, won an Oscar for her performance

pigeon'. Even more might you wonder about Charley's death, a harsh way to treat your right-hand-man, even as a warning to his brother – especially if the latter's as unimportant as Friendly insists. You might also be curious as to why a truck tries to run Terry down *before* he's discovered his brother's corpse; and you might also query the shot of 'Mr Big' watching the Commission on television – a device going back to Capra if not before.

The faults were generally overlooked, though later, in *Sight & Sound*, Lindsay Anderson called it 'a bad film' and made a bitter and well-aimed attack on the fascist implications of the final sequence – points which might have had more authority if he hadn't lauded at its expense a vastly inferior movie, *Force of Evil*, directed by Abraham Polonsky (who had been black-listed; Kazan, of course, was employed, successful and chic). Years later, Kazan commented that all Anderson 'had was this schematic left-wing idea about the ending', and, he pointed out, he had lived on the waterfront and Anderson hadn't.

The relentless dramatics would seem to have been Kazan's, rather than a mandate from Columbia or Spiegel; Kazan works in a coruscating style which is often momentarily stunning (as in the famous passage where important dialogue is lost under the ship's hooters) – and which is often offset by Boris Kaufman's grimy, grey photography of Hoboken across the river, with winter mists and winter steam drifting across the street; and that is offset again by Leonard Bernstein's jagged pre-'West Side Story' score, as emphatic as anything ever written for an Old-Dark-House thriller. The effect aimed at is the 'torn from today's headlines' sort of thing, which contradicts a weak-kneed preface intimating that such things happened in the past – and adding that the film 'will exemplify the way self-appointed tyrants can be defeated by right-minded

people in a vital democracy'. It will not, we find, indicate how the tyrants got there, and the man who defeats them is motivated rather by love (and later, revenge) than by convictions about democracy.

Brando's performance partly obscures this, just as it obscures the fact – for all the skill of his dialogue – that he's also having to enact out the old 'a man's gotta do what a man's gotta do' philosophy (there are other ways of showing an awakening conscience than this). It *is* a performance, so carefully thought out that there's nothing of Kowalski or Johnnie. He smiles a lot, a gentle, defenceless man, but, reprimanded, he does an insolent grin, the thug's form of defence when up against forces stronger. He's unthinking rather than vicious. He rolls his pug's eyes a lot in his battered face, as in the ring, sometimes in despair and sometimes not to miss anything – and both reactions have the same root cause: he's dumb, and he knows it. His eyes are more useful than his brain. He brings into play his hands when the words won't come. And for all that, Brando is still underplaying – or at least under-reacting – in marked contrast to the admittedly convincing histrionics of Malden and Cobb. The love scenes with Miss Saint he takes in a bantering, kidding fashion, in the way we might associate with Bogart or Melvyn Douglas, but in this sombre atmosphere they seem startlingly original, and are more holding than all the wham-bam-bam.

The performance brought awards from the New York critics, and the American and British Academies (it was Brando's third consecutive 'Best Foreign Actor' award from the British Film Academy: he had also won for *Viva Zapata!* and *Julius Caesar*). Miss Saint also won a (Best Supporting) Oscar; and the New York critics voted the film both the best of the year and Kazan the best director.

Brando's Oscar produced something like euphoria in Hollywood-watchers. In the first place, it was a just award; secondly, his good-humoured, tuxedoed acceptance suggested that he was falling comfortably into line with tradition; and thirdly, the accolade usefully carried with it increased power. No one nurtured in the place, voter or winner, is ever indifferent to the importance of Oscar, and the acumen so far shown by Brando might well grow into an influence. The public was showing an increasing tendency to go to the films the critics liked (in 1953, *Shane*, *From Here to Eternity*, *Moulin Rouge*), and the critics had liked all of Brando's films. The directors with whom he had worked – Zinnemann, Kazan, Mankiewicz, and to a lesser extent, Benedek – were the new Young Turks. With a handful of others – John Huston, George Stevens, Vincente Minnelli, and Kirk Douglas and Burt Lancaster among the actors – they were the long-awaited new leaders of the industry, not afraid of Harry Cohn, the big bad wolf, or anybody.

There was an infinitely lesser Brando film between the opening of *On the Waterfront* and the Oscar ceremonies nine months later, but it did not ruffle the climate of hopefulness, which was growing warmer all the while – despite a temporary chill when Brando announced that he was quitting films for ever to return to the stage. The climate already existed when 20th Century-Fox announced that Brando had signed an agreement with them, calling for two films a year. The details were left so vague (as published) as to suggest that the studio merely had first call on his services if they came up with a script he liked. He read the script of *The Egyptian* and agreed to do it – and that in itself is puzzling enough. The original novel was a long-winded account of people in antique times, in the manner (but without the gift) of Robert Graves; no one who has seen the film can imagine that at any stage there was a reasonably intelligent script; and the genre was one which seldom brought Hollywood any kudos. It was not the case that Brando needed a popular film after a solely 'artistic' success (a reason offered by Henry Fonda for some of the bad films he has made), though he may have been attracted to a complete turnabout. He may have felt that the character he would be playing was an interesting one, the sort he wouldn't be offered again (indeed not); but at all events, he changed his mind and retreated to New York, pleading illness. The film went ahead with the unfortunate Edmund Purdom, whose career was forever blighted by it; and 20th Century-Fox proceeded to load a breach-of-contract suit against Brando.

It was settled quickly enough: he would do *Désirée* instead. There was no indication that it would be a better film than *The Egyptian* – it was a version of an equally meretricious historical novel – but it would give him a chance to play Napoleon. Even poor actors don't resist such chances, even if the director

At the court of Napoleon, Brando as the emperor greets Talleyrand (John Hoyt) watched by Désirée (Jean Simmons) and Josephine (Merle Oberon)

was Henry Koster (who had done little worthwhile since his Deanna Durbin pictures) and the screenplay by Daniel Taradash (and they'd got his surname almost right). His performance gave the film its sole claim to distinction; he has the stances, the expressions, the appearance that we know from the iconography, and he is probably right in speaking softly but urgently – if too care-ful-ly. Napoleon must have been more magnetic: Brando's own magnetism had left him, as if drained by circumstances and the rest of the cast. Michael Rennie was a predictably wooden Bernadotte, Merle Oberon a colourless Josephine, and Jean Simmons a giggle-of-the-Fifth Désirée, or Daisy Ray, as the cast would have it.

It is Marseilles, France, 1794. Daisy Ray has met a certain Joseph Bonaparte (Cameron Mitchell) and has invited him home so that he may propose to her elder sister (Elizabeth Sellars). 'Bonaparte, what a curious name' says her brother. Two Bonaparte brothers arrive, and Napoleon takes Daisy Ray into the garden while the soundtrack gives with 'Parlez-moi d'Amour' and then the Marseillaise: 'Today' says Napoleon, 'that song is played throughout France. Tomorrow it will be heard throughout Europe.' But he has espoused the cause of Robespierre, and when he falls, is carted off to prison. 'An adventurer' says Daisy Ray's *frère*, 'that'll be the end of him.' How wrong he was! A moment later Napoleon is whistling the

Marseillaise under Daisy Ray's window, but the sensible puss refuses to elope with him.

Cut to Madame Tallyrand throwing a party; Daisy Ray, mysteriously in Paris, tries to gatecrash and is escorted in by Bernadotte, whose courtesy she repays by throwing a wineglass at Josephine on learning that she is Napoleon's intended. Her voice (she keeps a diary) details his rise to power, and then there's Josephine bidding her 'Welcome to Malmaison' (with, I have to interject, much less of the imperial grace than Loretta Young once loaned to the Empress Eugenie). Over dinner, Napoleon divulges his plans for Egypt, unheeding the steady good sense of Bernadotte. Bernadotte marries Daisy Ray, who has a baby. Enter Josephine, with long-stemmed roses from her garden. 'I envy you your roses' says Daisy Ray. 'I envy you your son' replies Josephine sadly. Napoleon becomes First Consul and then Emperor of the French ('Remember that first night he came to Marseilles?' says Elizabeth Sellars, a lady given – in this film – to stating the obvious).

So much has happened in just forty-five minutes, but the film dallies ten minutes on rehearsals for the Coronation, after which it scurries again – to the dissolution of the marriage to Josephine. 'She's only eighteen, you know, that Marie-Louise' says someone. As in most films about Napoleon, Marie-Louise remains a distant figure; here, it is Daisy Ray beside him when he holds up the King of Naples to the court at Versailles. He detains her with a music box: 'This belonged to the last Austrian to inhabit these quarters. Please teach me to waltz.' Then arrive at the Bernadottes' royal messengers from Sweden, offering Bernadotte the Crown Prince-ship because he, Bernadotte, Marshall of France, is not subservient to Napoleon. Daisy Ray learns her first Swedish word ('Sköl') and Napoleon is furious. Says Bernadotte: 'I watched you juggle with the thrones of Europe . . .' adding (debatedly, the only good line in the film), 'Would you make me a greater man than yourself – by obliging me to refuse a crown?'

In fact, of course, Bernadotte was as much a pawn of Napoleon as any of his family, and his desertion of him, in alliance with England and Russia, is a matter of some fascination. The film will have none of it: it is concerned instead with whether Daisy Ray will make a good Crown Princess. There's a fairly good scene (by the standards of this sort of movie – the only scene which has, say, something of the hold of the Garbo–Charles Boyer Napoleon film) where Daisy Ray is reminded by Napoleon that as she is now royal and a foreign national she is permitted at the French court only by his tolerance.

After the Russian debacle (indicated here by a cheap montage), it is of course to her that Napoleon rushes, begging her to straighten things out with her husband. She refuses, and the next thing we know she's confiding in her diary the escape from Elba and the Battle of Waterloo. He imprisons himself at Malmaison, and it is she who persuades him to surrender: Brando's musings on his plans for Europe might just – at this eleventh hour – have got this film off the ground, but we're distracted by a hideously painted back-cloth. One is left, simply, with surprise, at a last touch of intelligence. 'When did you stop loving me?' he asks. 'I don't know' she replies. As far as this film is concerned, most people never started.

The film was the antithesis of what was expected of Brando; it was filed away under the 'we all make mistakes' category, and quickly forgotten. Somehow, it did well financially, just edged out of the top ten money-making films of the year; it did better than *On the Waterfront*, and the success of both films brought Brando in at 10th in the *Motion Picture Herald*'s poll of top-drawing stars (1954). This fact had much to do with Sam Goldwyn's casting him in *Guys and Dolls*.

As a stage musical, this had opened on Broadway in 1950, an adaptation by Jo Swerling and Abe Burrows of a story ('The Idyll of Sarah Brown') by Damon Runyon, with music and lyrics by Frank Loesser, notable even among the incredibly good scores of the time. The show was a smash, and Hollywood bidding began. Paramount were so sure that they had it that they announced their cast – Betty Grable, Jane Russell and Bob Hope, with the ladies getting $150,000 apiece. Later, William Goetz (agent and sometime producer) said that Miss Russell owned half the rights. M-G-M bid $600,000 and Goldwyn bettered that offer by $50,000; in the end, the price was $800,000 plus residuals (not quite a record price). Goldwyn, once the most prolific of independent producers, had virtually ceased activity, but the success of a Technicolor musical in 1952 – *Hans Christian Anderson* – had given him a taste for making spectaculars the whole world would want to see, supposedly Hollywood entertainment at its glittering best. *Guys and Dolls* was budgeted at a huge $5 million. Joseph L. Mankiewicz was signed to adapt and direct; from the show came Vivian Blaine, a one-time Hollywood name who couldn't be bettered in the role, and Stubby Kaye. Jean Simmons would play the female lead, a New York mission sergeant who falls for a gambler, Sky Masterson. Frank Sinatra, his career on the upgrade, would be Nathan, gambler and long-time fiancé of Miss Adelaide (Miss Blaine). Brando would be Sky.

Goldwyn had originally negotiated with M-G-M for Gene Kelly, but they wouldn't release him (ironically, for he later signed an agreement with M-G-M to release, rather than his usual distributor, R.K.O.). The idea of Brando as a song-and-dance man was a novel one, not least to the actor himself. Having extracted a salary of $200,000 he agreed to have a go.

There was a smugness about the press releases during the filming. The screens had been heavy with adaptations of much-loved Broadway musicals (*The King and I* was the most recent) and Goldwyn's was bound to be the best. In the event, money or something was over-lavished: the film was interminable and fatally lacking in spontaneity. Mankiewicz had rewritten chunks of the book, and as in earlier films, showed a marked indulgence for his own words; the songs were packaged between endless Runyonesque conversations. His direction was prosaic, except in one sequence, where Sky takes Sarah on a jaunt to Havana and it briefly finds the correct verve. Most fatally, someone had decided on a stylized, representational New York, an unsuitable setting for Runyon's urban fairy-tale, which needs the clutter and clatter of a real, large, dusty, city.

The score and the stars did the salvage work. Miss Simmons received the best notices, for mingling gravity and an irrepressible gaiety as a serious girl unwillingly falling in love. Miss Blaine was praised again for her chorus-girl of genteel vulgarity, but Sinatra, in an over-sized Homburg, only registered when he sang. He later described Brando as 'the most overrated actor in the world', and their relations were not tempered by the fact that Sinatra preferred to work quickly, in one take if possible, and Brando was never in a hurry to get to the best take. Whatever the reason, Sinatra was overshadowed by Brando, despite the fact that his three songs (two solos and a duet with Miss Simmons) revealed him as no great singing shakes (an extended-play 45 r.p.m. record was issued; Sinatra's commitments to another record company prevented a full soundtrack album). Brando 'acted' his songs, and otherwise assumed without effort the character of Sky, insolently aware of his own sex-appeal, casually cunning and dandy-smart. Miss Simmons's singing voice was only marginally better, and their scenes together sometimes reflected a hint of amateurism which added, rather than detracted, from their charm. Brando later said that they had enjoyed making it, 'not having to be perfection, just doing a good days' work'.

Audiences at least were impressed. As the film played its dates throughout the following year (1956), it wound up second biggest attraction at American cinemas (following *Giant*). At the end of 1955, Brando made another appearance in the *Motion Picture Herald* poll of exhibitors, at 6th. Ahead of him, of the actors, were James Stewart, John Wayne, William Holden and Gary Cooper, and in a poll held by *Box-Office* magazine some months later, Holden was the only actor in front; in other words, with the exception of Holden (and his versatility had never been a byword), Brando was the best possible bet for any producer who needed a young star actor.

It is not surprising that M-G-M came after him for another film of a Broadway success, *The Teahouse of the August Moon*, although it was first announced that David Wayne would repeat his New York performance. The role was the sort of

Guys and Dolls, Sam
Goldwyn's version of a hit
Broadway musical : Jean
Simmons and Brando

challenge one expected Brando to pick up: that of Sakini,
Japanese interpreter and Okinawan houseboy – but as soon as
the credits are over and he turns to the audience you know that
the rest of it isn't going to differ much from what went on on
the boards of the Music Box. It had won a Pulitzer Prize and
the New York Drama Critics' Circle award – also, presumably,
it had delighted millions – so M-G-M and the director, Daniel
Mann, offered it infinite respect.

One didn't go to comedies at that time expecting smart or
funny dialogue, and the most this one offered was a bumbling
charm; the least was some poor colour and much expendable
talk. They'd used CinemaScope, and the long takes only
served to emphasise the staginess of it all. The humour was
supposed to spring from the contrast between the efficient and
sophisticated Americans and the primitive but resourceful
villagers, who, led by Brando as Sakini, continually outsmart
and outwit them. It wasn't an original idea, but John Patrick's
screenplay (based on his play, in turn taken from a novel by
Vern Sneider) had an agreeably sharp eye for certain military
personnel. The whole enterprise involving Sakini and the
woefully incompetent Captain Fisby (Glenn Ford), 're-
habilitating' a native village, is the brainchild of a malignly
stupid colonel who lives by the book (Paul Ford, playing
beautifully), and it does offer certain pleasures. The colonel's
discovery that they've thrown away the book, that Fisby's

countenanced a brandy still among the cottage-industries as well as a teahouse, is predictable, but none-the-less funny: he wanted to leave the army a brigadier, he tells Fisby, but now he'll be lucky to leave it a private; he wanted it for his wife – 'Fisby, you've broken the heart of a proud woman.'

The Teahouse of the August Moon: Brando, Paul Ford, so very funny as the Colonel, and Glenn Ford

The film should have ended there, but Fisby, earlier said to have personally delayed victory by a year, has to turn out to be a success; and he has to have a parting with Lotus Blossom (played by Machiko Kyo), which takes on all sorts of spiritual resonances, East and West and all that. In a pinewood setting left over, I imagine, from *Seven Brides for Seven Brothers*, they try for magic: they don't get it, or whatever they're after (it can be done, cf. Renoir's *The River* and Ivory's *Shakespeare Wallah*, both of which managed something about Westerners confronted with the East), and the comic mood is shattered. No one had tried to re-create this *Teahouse* for the screen; whatever the vigour and self-sufficiency promoted by Brando's earlier films – and they had been thought influential – Hollywood had become timorous, with no higher ambition than to set down replicas of successful Broadway theatre.

Brando's role was subsidiary to Glenn Ford's, and it's a tour de force of characterization. Having got the make-up right, and, I'm assured, the correct accent for an Okinawan speaking English, there's no acting to do: Sakini is sly and lazy, and he's adept at blandly stone-walling, and that's that.

While the public flocked to the *Teahouse*, those who hoped that Brando would transform American films did not entirely despair, for he had formed his own production company and ambitious plans were afoot. He said: 'I've made enough money to live comfortably the rest of my life, so my main concern is not with making money. I would like to make a cultural contribution and help some of the big social problems of our day.' He made that statement in 1957, while struggling with various projects he hoped to produce. Before looking at them, let us glance back to some other plans, and, for the record, to his first well-publicized romance.

In the autumn of 1954, it was announced in France that he would marry Josanne Berenger of Bandol, a resort on the Riviera; they had met in New York, and romance hastened when he visited her in the Midi. The world's press carried pictures of the engaged couple smiling at the cameras, but after much mystification and prevarication the wedding was called off, because, it was said, the prospective groom thought the prospective bride spoke too much to the press.

That Brando was a Francophile was witnessed by another French film project, when, after completing *Désirée*, he was interested in *L'Amant de Lady Chatterly*, to co-star Danielle Darrieux and Leo Genn, directed by Marc Allégret. He would, of course, have played the gamekeeper, but even though he offered to take a much reduced salary, the producers still couldn't arrive at that (the role was played by Erno Crisa). In 1955, Stanley Kramer announced that he would co-star with Cary Grant (once the most vocal of Brando's critics) and Sophia Loren in *The Pride and the Passion*, a tale of the Peninsula War: Kramer had to make do with a miscast Frank Sinatra. He was also 'definitely set' for *Heaven Knows, Mr Allison*, as was, at another point, Clark Gable; the role was finally played by Robert Mitchum.

His own production company, Pennebaker Productions, was named after his mother; his father, who had cleverly invested his earnings for him, was one of his business partners. The first film would be *To Tame a Land*, from a best-selling Western novel, with Brando starring and producing, and Robert Parrish directing. Paramount would release, and Brando would keep 85 per cent of the profits (Hollywood gasped: but hadn't a lesser star, Robert Mitchum, just got 75 per cent for a minor effort, *Foreign Intrigue*?). Due to script troubles, it was cancelled a year later, in 1956. The second project was also scrapped – after, again, much anticipatory publicity from Paramount: an adventure story about a United Nations research worker who disappears in South East Asia. The film would contain a fair amount of propaganda for the U.N. Technical Assistance Programme, and would be filmed on location throughout the area, with a script by Stewart Stern, produced by George Englund. In

1955, Brando optioned a story about a baseball player who wore spectacles, 'Man on Spikes'. In 1957, three more projects were announced: *Ride Comanchero* (later called *The Comancheros* and *Comanchero*), in which Brando would play a Mexican, in a story set towards the end of the last century; *Hang Me High*, which he would produce only; and *The Spellbinder*, for which he had reputedly signed Errol Flynn. One of the more persistent Pennebaker projects was *A Burst of Vermilion*, a Western which Brando himself was writing, but that got nowhere. Something called *Tiger on a Kite* was also planned, and in 1958 the title *Guns Up* first appeared. That eventually became *One-Eyed Jacks*.

As each project stalled, Brando was forced back into working for others – or almost: *Sayonara* was produced jointly by William Goetz (returning to film production) and Pennebaker. Warner Bros distributed, and they and Goetz were the guiding spirits behind the enterprise. Brando originally turned it down, but four factors changed his mind: the chance to return to Japan, which he had enjoyed both during the location work on *Teahouse* and an earlier visit to perfect his Okinawan accent – and Warners were paying not only his expenses but those of his entourage; a chance to work with Joshua Logan, a stage director who had just had two film successes, *Bus Stop* and *Picnic*; a salary of $300,000 plus a percentage; and a script with some points to make about racial intolerance. The screenplay was by Paul Osborn, based on a novel by James A. Michener, and it concerns the American military in Japan, their fraternizations, and the obstacles which the U.S.A.F. authorities put in the way of mixed marriages. It was strictly partisan (doesn't the whole world love a lover?) and already outdated (the regulations had been relaxed, the Japanese G.I. brides were already arriving in the States), but it did, for whatever reason, conform to Warner Bros long-standing policy of expounding liberal virtues.

Brando played Major Gruver, suffering from combat fatigue in Korea, and sent to Japan to be near his fiancée, Eileen (Patricia Owens), the daughter of General Webster (Kent Smith). Reluctantly and rashly he agrees to be best man at the wedding of an airman, Kelly (Red Buttons), to a local girl, Katsumi (Myoshi Umeki), and when he himself falls in love with a Japanese actress, Hana-ogi (Miiko Taka), he espouses the cause of mixed marriages. This results in plenty-trouble with his fiancée's family, and when he fails to persuade the general to countermand an order posting Kelly home to the States, Kelly and wife carry out a suicide pact. Because of this, Hana-ogi gives up Gruver, but (in a reversal of Michener's ending) he persuades her to marry him.

Brando was soon disillusioned about the film's attempt to say anything worthwhile on the subject of racial discrimination, and indeed in Britain it was dismissed as trite (it was

much better received by U.S. critics). Its main value was its picture of American servicemen abroad, done with an authenticity which was almost unchallengeable. For the rest, it was a long (very: almost 2½ hours) romantic wallow, with love and yearning all over the place. As in his two previous pictures, all else gave way before the director's determination to be passionate, visually striking and significant always and all at the same time. Verily, Japan was pretty, and the whole bright package deserved the title-song (by Irving Berlin, no less). Other than that, only Brando's presence gave it any relevance. His romantic interest, Miss Taka, had had no previous acting experience, and she resembled, in more ways than one, a block of wood; but Brando managed a more than passable impression of a man in love. The role was conventional, and he knew it; he gave one of his least showy performances as this mild, somewhat droll Texan (in the book, a Westerner), suggesting kindnesses and considerations only hinted at in the script and otherwise ignored by the director.

Sayonara opened in December 1957, to be followed five months later by *The Young Lions*, which Brando made for 20th Century-Fox after getting control over his portion of the script and a salary agreement of $200,000. Again, it was well-received by most of the press, and the public went to both films: both wound up among the dozen big financial successes of the year, and Brando trailed only Glenn Ford, Elizabeth Taylor and Jerry Lewis in the *Motion Picture Herald* poll of exhibitors. As it happened, 1958 would be his best year professionally since he won the Academy Award: it was also the last good year for a very long time. *Sayonara* was his tenth film, and would mark his fifth Oscar nomination – but that would also be his last in a long while.

Privately, things did not go well. In October 1957, he married an Indian actress, Anna Kashfi. At least, she looked Indian, and presumably Brando thought she was, for the marriage was over as soon as you could say Joan O'Callaghan, which was her real name – as revealed to the world by her proud Welsh parents the day after the wedding. A son was born, Christian Devi, in May 1958, and Miss Kashfi divorced Brando almost a year later, charging mental cruelty. Years later, she said: 'He wasn't a considerate husband or lover. I was young and immature and fascinated by [him] because he was a movie star'; the marriage, she said, died of boredom on both sides. On other occasions, she said that Brando was vindictive towards the women he had loved, and that he was the most egocentric man that ever lived.

The wedding pictures showed him with his hair dyed blond for *The Young Lions*, in which he played a German army officer. The film was based on Irwin Shaw's novel, a book very conscious of its own importance – a three-pronged tale of one German and two Americans, tracing their fates through the

Sayonara: At the bazaar:
Miiko Taka and Brando

1939–45 war. Shaw's best talent was irony, and that was retained in Edward Anhalt's screenplay, a synthesis of the experience of war in best-seller terms. On those terms it is entertaining (as Brando expressly hoped when considering it: 'They say in Hollywood if you want messages you go to Western Union. People are not interested in the message picture, but entertainment. I believe a combination of both is possible and essential, particularly in the international exchange of ideas.') It revives much better than *From Here to Eternity*, based on a better book, with a better director (Zinnemann), and considered at the time to be much superior. Once you get used to being hurtled back and forth between the German and the Americans, the incidents prove lively; and Edward Dmytryk, directing, keeps things running smoothly from myriad and varied locations.

Brando plays Christian Diestl, part-time ski-instructor who's discovered spouting pro-Nazi sentiments to an American girl (Barbara Rush). She provides the link with the Americans, Whiteacre (Dean Martin), a Broadway singing-star (in the book, a writer), and Noah (Montgomery Clift). They are both about to join the army, but Noah meets a girl, Hope (Hope Lange), and the film dallies on her father's prejudice when he learns that Noah is a Jew. The action reverts to Christian, and not a moment too soon; last seen as an officer in occupied Paris, he's in Berlin on an errand for his friend and commander, Hardenberg (Maximilian Schell), delivering a gift to his wife (May Britt). She leaves him in her flat to dine with a general, and returns to find him drunk. The subsequent sexual fencing is splendidly done by Brando: she is so 'forward' that he is embarrassed, silent, not looking at her, seemingly abstracted. The director, Dmytryk, once observed that Clift was the clever one, and seemed not to be, and that Brando was stupid and pretended not to be: but Brando's playing here is more original than anything Clift ever did (in life, most people can't take overt sexual overtures, at least not from your best friend's wife; I can't think of another movie hero thus fazed).

Brando also brings something original to his next sequence, with Hardenberg in the desert, behind enemy lines, preparing to mow down a small British unit: both men go about the task with exhilaration, caution and wonder. Later, when they come across a survivor, Christian, less cold-blooded, refuses to shoot him; and Brando's expression as he waits for Hardenberg's shot is as enigmatic as anything Garbo ever managed – part contempt, part smiling embarrassment, part the conceit of a man who thinks he understands humanity. After that, his smug Nazi, beautifully and correctly accented, is less interesting: he is an idealist with wrong ideals reduced to impotency and despair. No one, including Brando himself, seems interested in the later, disillusioned Christian – but this may

Previous page: Brando behind the camera for his first film as director: *One-Eyed Jacks*

Left: Brando as the German officer in *The Young Lions* (the film was not in colour)

be because the character has been softened in his journey from book to screen.

Reverting to the Americans, the film gets mealy-mouthed about anti-semitism in the army. Noah gets picked on (just as Clift was, earlier, in *From Here to Eternity*), and we have to assume it's because he's Jewish. He's called 'dogface', and his sadistic captain hurls away his copy of 'Ulysses'. Whiteacre gets posted away for pointing out that the man is being victimized, but Noah still gets beaten to a pulp and stuck in the jug. Coming out, he finds his old enemies have clubbed together to return his stolen money and to replace the book; and as the sadistic officer has also been exposed, you have to conclude that the army isn't so bad after all.

The film is charged with this sort of elementary drama. The reason that *From Here to Eternity* now fails is that the observation in the book was from life, not from other books; Hollywood bowdlerized and conventionalized it. In the four years between these two films, censorship was relaxed, but Shaw had written precisely the sort of second-remove stuff which Hollywood understands best. You don't want to throw-up when the Jew becomes a hero (rescuing one of his erstwhile torturers), because it's exactly what you expect. As for the final scenes, the opening-up of the concentration camp, I think we should be grateful to any movie that treats that subject honourably. We are still contending with Shaw's heavy irony, but one senses the indignation of the film's makers at this point, and their awareness of their limitations. There is an odd look, a look of seriousness, on the faces of Noah and Whiteacre as they refer to the 'ovens' – after which they run across Christian and shoot him down, just in time for Noah to return to Brooklyn and Hope.

Martin acts with a fatcat smile which suits his interpretation of the role; Clift is as sympathetic as he was in *Eternity*; and Schell is good as the career officer. It is possible that he and Brando were hoping to say something about the lack of humanness, the lack of humanity that one finds in many Germans, but, clearly, this wasn't the film to do it. If so, it would be indicative of Brando's complete complicity in a role, because one of the reasons that Christian was softened for the screen was that Brando did not want to make a point of the Nazis being solely responsible for the war; and, probably, he did not want to see Clift and Martin get all the sympathy that was going. Sam Peckinpah, who worked for a while on *One-Eyed Jacks*, spoke much later about Brando in that film: 'Strange man, Marlon. Always doing a number about his screen image, about how audiences would not accept him as a thief, how audiences would only accept him as a fallen sinner – someone they could love.' Brando held a similar view of Christian, and he was anxious, at the end, that his dead body be spread-eagled in the manner of the Crucifixion, but Clift, in

The Young Lions: Brando and Max Schell, who played his friend and commanding officer

the only scene they shared together, violently opposed the notion and it was dropped. In an interview in *Films Illustrated*, Dmytryk spoke of both actors: Clift, he said, 'hated the way Marlon acted, disliked the whole Actors' Studio approach. With Monty Take 1 was the best . . . you could never go beyond Take 3 or 4 because Monty would have to rest and come back fresh to it, whereas Marlon didn't get going till about Take 40, because he didn't know what he was doing. If they had had to work together it would have been impossible. Glenn Ford had the same trouble with Marlon on *Teahouse of the August Moon*. Ford would come in first time, and by the time Marlon was ready, Ford was all washed out. All the same, I must say that when Marlon does get to Take 40, he's wonderful. He told me after we had finished *The Young Lions* that it was the best working relationship he had had since Elia Kazan, who is his spiritual godfather. But we had a test of strength before the film began. This is not uncommon with certain types of actor, but it has to be faced and got out of the way or the film will suffer.'

Chronologically, Dmytryk is the first of Brando's directors to suggest difficulties, though Joshua Logan, also speaking retrospectively, does hint that he had to exercise some diplomacy during *Sayonara*: 'The greatest natural talent of our time. A special sort of man with a special sort of possibilities. He can act anything. His complex is that he thinks everyone wants to put him down. He hates authority. He'll defy anyone with power – producers, directors, writers, politicians. He has only confidence in those who are poor and anonymous.'

**9 TRAVAIL:
ONE MINOR
TWO MAJOR**

While Pennebaker struggled to find the right script, it agreed to partner Martin Jurow and Richard A. Shepherd in a venture which United Artists would distribute – the film of a play by Tennessee Williams. It had started out as 'Battle of Angels', his first full-length play; after a disastrous out-of-town opening, it had been abandoned – by all except Williams, who was wont to re-work material. The new version, much changed, was called 'Orpheus Descending', and the leading roles were fashioned with Brando and Anna Magnani in mind (indeed, Williams once said that after *Streetcar*, every one of his chief male roles was written for Brando). Both declined them, and the play was done on Broadway by Cliff Robertson and Maureen Stapleton, with medium success, in 1957. Williams continued to dicker with the play, and Meade Roberts was brought in to work on the screenplay; Williams persisted with Brando, and the film finally got made – as *The Fugitive Kind*, directed by Sidney Lumet, who had established a reliable talent since coming from television two years earlier.

No one could blame Brando for being wary of the material. His role was that of a drifter, Val Xavier, a strolling guitarist who had been run out of every town he'd ever played in. He lands in a Mississippi town called Two Rivers, and gets a job in the general store, run by Lady Torrance (Anna Magnani). He settles down, and they fall in love, a matter suspected by the husband dying of cancer upstairs. Val is simultaneously sought by Carol Cutrere (Joanne Woodward), of the town's first family, but because of dipso and nympho tendencies as much of an outcast as he. The husband, Jeb, learns that Lady is pregnant by Val, and he sets fire to the confectionary parlour she and Val had built. She shoots Jeb and he dies; and the sheriff and the townsfolk drive Val into the fire with the hose-pipes. Later, in the ashes, Carol finds his snakeskin jacket.

It began, strikingly, with Brando listening insolently to his enemies, heard but unseen. His power in this prologue pervades the subsequent events, imbuing the character with something more than Williams had written into it – the quintessential Williams hero nevertheless, glowering, idealistic-disillusioned, oddly quixotic, possibly bisexual. Brando's excellence was equalled by Magnani, Miss Woodward and Miss Stapleton (now playing the sheriff's wife), three others not conforming to the standards of bigoted society, pitilessly mouldering. The conclusion, however, was not positive: Williams still hadn't got the thing right.

The peripheries of the tale are as over-heated as its centre, but, like most of Williams's work, it is not as absurd as its outline. His stuff is not easy to film: the melodramatic essentials, the sexual exoticism, the poetic yearnings must be rendered exactly and appropriately. Kazan had succeeded twice, compellingly (*Streetcar* and *Baby Doll*), but other direc-

Left: *The Fugitive Kind*, the second version of Tennessee Williams' *Orpheus Descending*: Brando, Anna Magnani and Joanne Woodward. The French title was *L'Homme a la peau de Serpent* (The Man with the Snakeskin)

tors, before and after *The Fugitive Kind*, either over-heightened Williams or steel-filed him down. John Huston was to find the right approach with *The Night of the Iguana*, and Lumet found it here: the exact boldness, the exact black-and-whiteness. Both judged the extents to which the photographer (here, Boris Kaufman) could load the screen and the players the dialogue. It may be a matter of chance: Lumet's direction was effusive, with too many hints, ends dangling, and the evil of the play now merely implied; but the effect was of some modern myth, its curling edges unfamiliar. The public was not comfortable with it; the reviews and attendance were on the good side of modest.

It had not been filmed, incidentally, near the Mississippi, but in upstate New York, in an atmosphere of mutual aggression between Brando and Magnani: the expressed delight in working together had gone within days. The gossip was that Brando had made an unsuccessful pass at Magnani, and revenged himself on her by behaving as rudely as possible – and she was not a lady to let an insult pass lightly.

The atmosphere on Brando's own production, at last under way, was no happier. Stanley Kubrick, hired as director on the strength of his first important film, *Paths of Glory*, realized that only one man would have autonomy, and departed before filming began. The nominal producer was Frank P. Rosenberg, who had brought the property to Brando, a novel called 'The Authentic Death of Henry Jones' by Charles Neider. Neider's own screenplay was rejected, and the final one was credited to Guy Trosper and Calder Willingham. Brando himself, after some deliberation, replaced Kubrick as director, and proceeded to go out of control.

There were endless re-takes, hold-ups for the right climatic effects, delays while he decided what to do next. The budget, originally fixed at $1,800,000, went to over $5 million, and the actual shooting extended to over six months. Trouble didn't cease when the cameras stopped turning: the first cut lasted over five hours. One hour was chopped out without great difficulty, but Paramount was no more interested in a four-hour film than a five-hour one: it came out finally at two hours twenty minutes. The company's trepidation was somewhat alleviated by the world-wide interest, and the ease with which the publicity department could get news coverage.

Brando's Western: *One-Eyed Jacks*. (The title was inaccurate: 'You're a one-eyed jack around here, Dad, I seen the other side of your face', Brando says to Karl Malden, but Malden was the *only* character who wasn't what he seemed, who could be accused of duplicity.) He had insisted that the film was a frontal attack on the clichés of the genre – but even the most respectful critics told him that it wasn't. His performance was: you'd have to go back to William S. Hart to find a Western hero

One-Eyed Jacks: Brando as the hero (the ace of hearts indicates that the painting is not original)

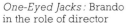

One-Eyed Jacks: Brando
in the role of director

so lacking in heroic qualities. This one was vain, vicious, cunning, sentimental, and, whether intended or not, rather stupid. Brando was perhaps confused between the performance and the film. He exists, therefore the film exists, and they are one and indivisible. The esteem accorded him justifies the film, but he neglected something in his performance, often a matter of brooding Napoleonic silences in close-up. For the first time he seemed to be repeating himself. The director's fascination with his leading actor often looks like megalomania.

The film, like its hero, was vain, vicious, cunning and sentimental, and you could say beautiful and perverted as well. It borrows from John Ford (the town fiesta, the sandstorm), and from Japanese cinema (the beguiling silences, the seascapes), and, like *Viva Zapata!* meanders from the realistic to the romantic and back. Its self-indulgence, rare at the time, would be echoed and exceeded in scores of lesser films before the decade was out, so that the symbolism of Brando's use of himself now seem tentative. Reservations remain about the sadism, the first confirmation of Brando's Messiah-complex – but that got more extensive workings-over in later films over which he nominally had less control. Here, at least, his whipping by Malden could be justified by the fact that Brando had fallen for his step-daughter – and it gave him a motivation to keep his vengeance at white-hot pitch.

The film is built around revenge, and it's a good motif for a Western. Rio (Brando) and Dad Longworth (Malden) are bank-robbers stranded in the desert with one horse. Longworth goes for another and doesn't return; Rio surrenders to his pursuers. Longworth, in fact, had good grounds for not returning – he knew it would be hopeless: but when they meet again, he lies and says there were no horses available. By this time, he's respectable, over the border, the sheriff of Monterey. Rio arrives, bent on revenge, and also to rob the bank with three companions – the Mexican (Larry Duran), who had been his jail companion, and two drifters (Ben Johnson and Sam Gilman). In self-defence, he kills a drunken reveller who had been pestering a woman, and Longworth, who had welcomed him, if gingerly, not long before, horse-whips him and runs him out of town.

Now: Rio's action should have made him the hero of the hour – there were enough witnesses; and as an old pal of the sheriff, he might have been immune from justice. So here's a credible dilemma being handled in conventional movie manner so that the plot can function. Longworth does have reasons for wanting Rio out of the way – he has betrayed him, he has betrayed the Code of the West (it doesn't matter that Rio knows of his past: so do the townsfolk). As the film proceeds, Longworth – though played in Malden's usual smug, vacillating way – becomes even more dastardly, and Rio even more noble. His faults are played down, though at the end, he betrays the Code and shoots Longworth in the back (as did Robert Taylor in the 1941 *Billy the Kid*, which also talked much of the Code and also attempted a compendium of all Western myths).

The bank raid goes wrong. Because of the girl – Longworth's wife's niece (Pina Pellicier, a Mexican 'discovered' for the film, and a suicide some years later) – Rio has opted out. The Mexican refuses to accompany the other two, and they kill him (with overtones of racialism). They proceed alone and bungle it: one is killed, and so is a small girl. The sheriff rounds up Rio and leads the townsfolk in refusing to believe his innocence. The West was a place of rough justice; and though Monterey is picturesque, and civilized by the standards of other towns, you can almost smell the blood.

For all its romanticism, this was the first Western in fifty years to broach realism: squalid girls in empty, run-down bars, the men in duds like those of the photographs of the period (1880). There are few characters in any Western (till Peckinpah's, later) as wholly despicable as the deputy (Slim Pickens), a rube-like yokel who guards Rio and spitefully ridicules him. The two bandits, though first discovered when one of them is manhandling a whore, may well be homosexual; and the girl is exactly the sort of grave, meek thing to attract the sort of man Rio is. There is, in fact, so much in the movie that is good that one would like to see the footage left on the cutting-room floor.

At the box office, *One-Eyed Jacks* performed respectably and, via eventual television showings, earned back its cost. Brando's debut as a director was decreed promising (it was more than that), but it's a fair bet that he was never asked to direct again. Little more was heard of Pennebaker and his plans to produce, as if, having given birth to a monster, the effort had depleted him for life. He would, nevertheless, have artistic control over his next film, beside which the production troubles of *One-Eyed Jacks* are small fry.

This was a refloating of the Bounty, M-G-M's old warhorse of 1935. The original *Mutiny on the Bounty* had won an Oscar for the Best Picture way back then, and had been enormously popular; there had been a number of reissues. The decision to remake it (a suggestion by John Sturges, the director) in Technicolor and wide-screen was probably taken from necessity rather than zeal (if either quality is at a premium in Hollywood): M-G-M needed a big, splashy picture. A year earlier, the studio's deficit had been wiped out by the remake of an old property, *Ben Hur*, and it was hoped that as many people might turn up for a second sortie of the Bounty mutineers. The production was assigned to Aaron Rosenberg, who had moved to Metro after a successful ten years at Universal (albeit that his first two pictures for his new company flopped). On the principle that for the biggest pictures you get the biggest stars, however unlikely, Brando was approached to play either Clark Gable's old role, that of Fletcher Christian, leader of the mutineers, or that of Charles Laughton, the villainous and wronged Captain Bligh. He turned down both suggestions (unlike Laughton, Olivier, Bette Davis and the other few movie-stars working in traditional actors' fashion, he has never played a real villain), and he turned down the film again when he read Eric Ambler's script. Each time M-G-M cajoled him, their terms became more generous; in their anxiety to get him, they promised him a good proportion of the earth, if not the moon. He eventually indicated that he was not much interested in the voyage of the Bounty, but he was drawn to the

Mutiny on the Bounty:
Brando with Tarita who
was sort-of his wife in the
film—and later on in life

fate of the survivors on Pitcairn Island. He had re-read the
original novel by Nordhoff and Hall, and was fascinated to
learn that the mutineers, instead of finding happiness in their
Pacific paradise, had killed each other off. Rosenberg, in his
own words, 'made a deal agreeing to give him consultation
rights on that part of the picture'.

Brando's salary was $500,000 against 10 per cent of the
gross, plus $5,000 a day overtime if shooting went over
schedule. His eventual overtime take was estimated at figures
varying from $750,000 to $1,250,000, and the costs escalated
from an agreed $10 million to over $19 million, easily the most
expensive film yet made.

The *Mutiny* again : Brando and Trevor Howard—Fletcher Christian and Captain Bligh, famous names in movie mythology

His intransigence over the ending of the film was not its sole difficulty. There was trouble with the reconstructed Bounty on its voyage to the Tahitian locations, which were thus about to be utilized as the rainy season started. Ambler's script had been reworked by Borden Chase and William L. Driscoll, but the final credit went to Charles Lederer. In December 1961, after two months' shooting, Brando decided that he wanted to switch roles and play the botanist (which Richard Haydn was playing). It was at that point that Carol Reed, who was directing, left, and was replaced by Lewis Milestone. In 'The Celluloid Muse', Milestone spoke of the experience: 'I felt it would be quite an easy assignment because they'd been on it for months and there surely couldn't be much more to do. To my dismay, I discovered that all they'd done was a seven-minute scene just before they land in Papeete. . . . Brando swears that he had nothing to do with Carol Reed's departure; that was a matter between Reed and the producer. . . . During my first two weeks on the film Brando behaved himself and I got a lot of stuff done – especially with sequences like the arrival in Tahiti, when I could work with the British actors. I got on beautifully with Trevor Howard, Richard Harris, and the others; they were real human beings, and I had a lot of fun.

'Then the trouble started. I would say that what went basically wrong with *Mutiny on the Bounty* was that the producer made a number of promises which he subsequently couldn't keep. It was an impossible situation because, right or wrong, the man simply took charge of everything. You had the option of sitting and watching him or turning your back on him. Neither the producers nor I could do anything about it.

'Charlie Lederer wrote the script from day to day. He would bring it on the set in the morning, then they would go into Marlon Brando's dressing room and lock themselves up there till lunchtime . . .

'After lunch, they came out. By then it was about two-thirty and we hadn't shot a scene. You had the option of shooting it, but since Marlon Brando was going to supervise it anyway, I waited until someone yelled "Camera!", and went off to sit down somewhere and read the paper.'

Milestone, an old professional, believed that a director directed, and an actor took orders; he was not disposed towards Brando's technique, which was to get, well, first the right mood. With actor and director not speaking, Brando went into endless debates with the producer and the writer, till his relationship with both also deteriorated. Milestone reckons that Brando's behaviour 'cost the production at least $6 million', but whatever his prima donna conduct, he had been granted that control over the ending. He had seen in it a chance to offer a message to humanity, and he was not going to let it go. In the end, twelve different endings were written or shot, with the help of writers of the calibre of Billy Wilder and Ben Hecht.

Milestone might, in fairness, have acknowledged that Brando's methods were opposed to his own. Later, John Cassavetes said that when Brando was allegedly difficult it was because he was 'unsatisfied, often justifiably, with some aspect of the project he's on – the director, the script or whatever. But when those things are right, when people deal with him honestly, there's no one better – ask any actor.' Brando was not, after all, the first actor to submit the crew to his vagaries: in the late forties, for instance, at the height of their popularity, Bing Crosby disappeared to play golf, and Humphrey Bogart only filmed after lunch, using the morning for rehearsals and his jug of martinis; in the sixties, Gregory Peck liked only to film in the mornings. But none of these or other actors attracted the hostility that Brando did, which says much about his conduct. No one on the *Bounty* film had a good word to say for Brando, including Trevor Howard, a star himself, and one who had worked with dozens of big names quite happily; Richard Harris's comments were virulent. Brando sued *The Saturday Evening Post* for $4 million when it published a graphic account of the *Bounty* adventures, but the matter didn't come to court.

It was, alas, impossible to see the film without thinking of Brando's sulks. It turned out to be surprisingly good, but it never became the duel, the battle of giants required by the subject, a prolonged clash between hero and villain.

It starts well. Bligh (Trevor Howard) is a salty-looking man; it is his first captaincy, and he makes it clear that Christian (Brando) was not his first choice for First Officer. He refers to him as 'a career fop', and Christian irritates him by referring to their voyage as 'a grocery errand' – they're being sent to the South Seas by the West India Merchants to collect sprigs of breadfruit trees, with the idea of feeding the fruit to the slaves in the West Indies. Christian is a fop indeed, supercilious and smirking. Their first clash occurs when Mills (Richard Harris) is accused by a crew-mate of stealing cheese: Mills confesses that he acted at the captain's command, but Bligh refuses corroboration. He is a petty tyrant; he flinches when told that the men have a complaint, and when making absurd commands his look is furtive. He tries to go round the Horn to Tahiti, against advice, but is forced to turn back – Christian has countermanded his orders. The actual mutiny occurs because he has insisted on restricting the water supply (for the breadfruit plants), and put it, literally, out of reach. As a result, one man is keel-hauled, another drops to his death from the water jug and another goes mad after drinking sea water. It is Christian's compassion in offering the man water which brings Bligh's wrath on him, and thus to blows.

It doesn't matter how much of this is based on fact: these are strong situations, and both Brando and Howard are outstanding actors. But just as the film's publicity played up Brando and part-ignored Howard, so does the film, and that is one of its weaknesses. Their best exchange is when Bligh observes that Christian is motivated by only one thing – contempt; and Christian replies that he tries not to let his private opinion conflict with his duty. Howard is not so much fun as Laughton was, nor as loathsome, but his Blight is much more a flesh-and-blood being, a blunt, instinctive navy man.

For Gable's straightforward hero, Brando offers a man of complexity. Despite the permanent sneer, he commands sympathy from the start – and that is partly because his parody of a British aristocrat accent is done with wit; it is excessive and amusing. But if he gets his inflections correct, the voice is too 'light'; it's rather the voice of a poseur. He finally gets gummed up when he has to say to the native girl, the King's daughter (Tarita): 'My name is Fletcher Christian.' He can't avoid it being ridiculous. After two hours you're so sick of the accent and the mannerisms that he thinks characterize the British aristocracy that you long for Clark Gable, so that even if they'd given Howard more footage they would never have been equals, eagles both; and as a silly man who becomes a hero under duress it is quite wrong for this particular film.

For what the film is, is spectacle. There is nothing wrong with an attempt at profundity, but Brando's earlier reluctant heroes were part of weightier events. The scenes at sea – billowing sails and scrubbed decks, seascapes and twilights – are infallible film material. The Polynesian islands are magnificently photographed, and as a roadshow spectacle the scenes of native dances, native rituals and native fishing are entirely apt; the screen throbs, and no matter that it's all extraneous to the plot. But when this *Mutiny* goes on the jungle princess kick, halfway through, it sags, earthbound and ghastly. For all I know, Christian was ordered back because the king's daughter had taken a fancy to him, but it rings false, reeking of pre-Griffith two-reelers. Indeed, apart from the mutiny itself, the second half strays into muddy waters. The Court of Enquiry which exonerated Bligh is disposed of in three minutes. Twenty minutes or more are allotted to the settling on Pitcairn – a superfluous business with Christian muttering: 'I put it to you, we shall never find contentment on this island.' In the ending used (and it was a compromise one; the first, Ambler's, couldn't have been worse), he proposes to sail back to face the music, but his men loyally burn the Bounty: after trying to recover his sextant, he dies from burns. It concludes in bathos, and although Brando was not, finally, responsible, it is probable that without his participation a more simple and appropriate ending might have been found. (In fact, Christian was murdered two years after landing on Pitcairn by a native he had brought from Tahiti: to have told this truth would presumably have meant either a racial slur or showing Christian in a bad light.)

10 THE DECLINE BEGINS

Left: Brando as the
American Ambassador in
The Ugly American

Mutiny on the Bounty finally opened eighteen months after *One-Eyed Jacks*, in November 1962. Comment was favourable, and business: only three films took more money at the box office during the two-year period, but as the domestic gross (United States and Canada) amounted to $9 million, it will probably always remain in the red in the M-G-M ledgers. Its comparative success somewhat muffled industry critics, who wanted Brando thrown out of Hollywood, together with Elizabeth Taylor, because of her shenanigans on the *Cleopatra* set, and Marilyn Monroe, whose lateness caused hold-ups and finally cancellation of *Something's Gotta Give*.

Brando must have felt that much of his behaviour was justified when both *Jacks* and *Mutiny* were accorded good notices, but whether or not their production mistakes, and his own, taught him anything, it would be some years again before the outside world heard of his antics on the set. Very quietly he started a film at Universal, produced and directed by George Englund, with a screenplay by Stewart Stern, both of whom had been with him in Pennebaker. Indeed, the film had started as a Pennebaker production: *The Ugly American*, from a best-selling novel by William J. Lederer and Eugene Burdick. Brando and Englund had bought the rights for $100,000, and when they sold them to Universal (or Universal-International, as it then was), the price is reputed to have included the assets of Pennebaker, to the tune of a million dollars. Universal also got Brando to agree to a picture deal, but the company knew what it was doing, for it had been bought by M.C.A., Brando's agent. Its new head, Lew Wasserman, knew better than any-one what Brando was worth, and his long acquaintance with the actor should have ensured an agreement favourable to both parties. Wasserman agreed to let Englund direct, a debut: his inexperience was compensated for by Brando's high regard.

Englund did a good job on *The Ugly American*, notably managing some moments of alarm. What no one could buck was the nature of the political arguments set forth. In some quarters, the film, like the book, was greeted as a hard-speared attack on American foreign policy – and it does provide a sweeping, if confused, indictment of American interference in South East Asia. The level of argument is specious, and it nestles round a tired old plot about a duped American ambassador (Brando), and his wartime-buddy-now-a-nationalist leader, Deong (Eiji Okada), who may or may not be a tool of the Communists. The chief points about it were the Thai locations, and Brando's portrait of the ambassador, a decent but obstinate man, anxious to do good but going about it so naively as to bring about the destruction of his friend – and, of course, his own disillusionment. It was a new departure for him; he acquired a moustache for the role, and a pipe and spectacles, and was smoothly urbane – at least, in his public persona. In the scenes with his wife (Sandra Church) and

Deong, he played it doubtful and dishevelled. It was a typically astute way of playing a public man.

The film was moderately successful, and the star's metamorphosis from noisy, temperamental star back to serious actor was duly noted. His performance gave further credence to the theory that he could play anything, and admirers were further heartened by the announcement that his next film would be a comedy, *Bedtime Story*, directed by Ralph Levy, from television, at Universal, with Pennebaker listed as one of the co-producers.

Universal had been turning out a series of vaguely salacious comedies with players like Doris Day, Rock Hudson and Tony Curtis. The name of Stanley Shapiro appeared on most of them, as producer and/or writer, and he functioned on *Bedtime Story* as both, sharing the screenplay credit with Paul Henning. It was somewhat more abrasive than the others, and it would have been better still if they'd speeded things up and done some pruning – notably in the sequence where David Niven explains that he robs for philanthropic reasons and we visit said reasons.

Niven was Brando's own choice for co-star, and has one of his best roles. They play con-men. Niven has class and works the Côte d'Azur, where the chickens to be plucked are wealthy American women who think he's an exiled prince needing funds for his people. Brando is an army corporal stationed in Germany, and his victims are frauleins who think he is starving to pay for his grandmother's operation. It is only suggested that Niven beds his victims; Brando is cruder, and prepared to shed his uniform on any pretext. Demobbed, he meets Niven on a train, and fancies settling in his playground. Twice, Niven ships him out, till he learns too much and forces Niven into taking him into partnership. They continue to 'take' rich broads, with Niven posing as a prince till he's engaged to them, after which he introduces his idiot brother, Prince Ruprecht, who is Brando. They split, and for a while the piece zips along, cross and double-cross, as inventive as any of the thirties comedies on which it is modelled (there's a high point, believe it or not, when Niven crashes a whip down on Brando's supposedly paralysed legs); but then it goes slack and fizzles out, with Brando marrying an heiress who turns out to be a beauty queen (Shirley Jones).

The slapstick is similarly misjudged: Brando buried in the sand with a seagull on his head, Brando in a runaway wheelchair. Brando takes the script literally. Told he's crude by Niven, referred to by him as 'an uneducated, maladjusted army corporal' and by Niven's aide as 'an ape', his performance embodies each of these aspects, perhaps because he's too complete an actor to ignore them. His comedy technique, otherwise rudimentary, is at his best when he's being fastidious – giving his sad little spiel to his girlfriends, offering advice to

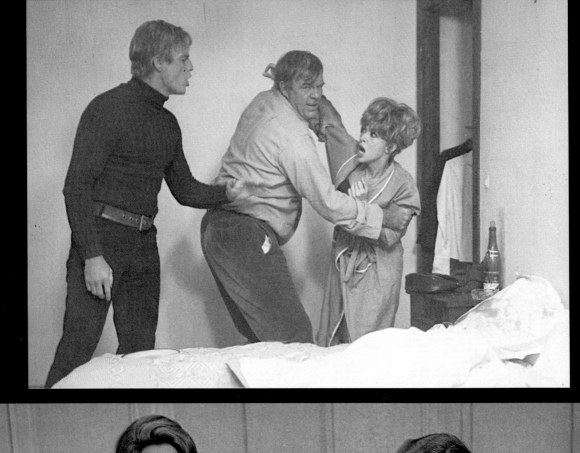

the more experienced Niven. Niven is quicker and much more debonair, but it is a complementary performance: the script has made sure of that.

Brando's next commitment was at 20th Century-Fox, for Aaron Rosenberg, who had left M-G-M after *Mutiny on the Bounty*. He signed Brando to play a German in a film called *Morituri*, with a screenplay by Daniel Taradash based on a novel by Werner Jörg Lüdecke, and directed by another German, Bernard Wicki. Brando was Crain, a pacifist and a man of some wealth, blackmailed by British Intelligence (in the person of Trevor Howard) into working for the Allies. Posing as a member of the Gestapo, he is to board a German cargo ship, and, in due time, disarm the scuttling charges so that, in evading capture, the captain can't sink it. (The Allies want the cargo – rubber.) Crain's adventures on board are considerable: the only real Nazi on board is the First Officer, whose help he has to enlist. The Captain (Yul Brynner) is anti-Nazi and therefore wary of Crain; two officers who board the ship – with a Jewish prisoner (Janet Margolin) – are suspicious and wire Gestapo headquarters. There is a mutiny, and the ship begins to sink – slowly; Crain and the Captain are left aboard, and Crain begins to work on the Captain's anti-Nazi feelings in order to radio to a nearby Allied vessel . . .

This is a good cliff-hanging plot, tense enough, and, as melodrama, attractive enough; its statements on Nazism, if unremarkable, would be worth repeating any time. Brando's own prerequisite, that a movie be more than a mindless entertainment, was reasonably fulfilled; among didactic thrillers there were many more didactic and less thrilling – like another shipboard drama which came out in 1965, Stanley Kramer's *Ship of Fools*. I mention that, because *Morituri* was mauled by the press, and it seemed to me then, and since, a decent entertainment – worth a dozen *Ships of Fools*, which Mr Bosley Crowther of *The New York Times* listed as one of the ten best pictures of the year. There are fashions in these things, and neither Brando nor the director were in vogue. Wicki had been much praised for *Die Brücke* when it was shown in the States in 1961, but he collected no roses when he directed *The Visit* for Fox in 1964 – though it had seemed to me that he had done a good job on that against almost insurmountable odds. Similarly, he gave a raw edge to the placid movie conventions of *Morituri*, setting up a conviction where the dialogue provided none. He was inestimably aided by Brando: with little character to work on, he again did an excellent German accent and conveyed with ease the tensions of the saboteur. The initial reaction was so poor that Fox hurriedly retitled it *The Saboteur, Code Name 'Morituri'*, but it still didn't do much business.

For his next role, Brando returned to Sam Spiegel, and Spiegel's productions are not, or are not intended to be, mind-

Left above : *The Night of the Following Day :* Brando, Jess Hahn, and Rita Moreno

Below : Ill-starred *Countess from Hong-Kong :* Brando and Sophia Loren, in tranquil mood

less. He tends to like 'class' subjects, usually with a literary flavour (since *On the Waterfront* they had included *The Strange One*, *The Bridge on the River Kwai*, *Suddenly Last Summer* and *Lawrence of Arabia*). You might say he showed some concern for the plight of man. He also made a habit of using praised and/or expensive talents. Here, he had Arthur Penn directing, and Lillian Hellman credited with the script (from a play and novel by Horton Foote). Later, Miss Hellman asked for her name to be removed, but there is question that they all regarded it as something more than roaring melodrama.

It is of the species small-town drama, Southern variety. Texas, in fact. At first you think of King's Row, but later descend to Peyton Place, with the expected cross-section, and how they react to the news that Bubber Reeves (Robert Redford) has broken jail. Most affected is his wife, Anna (Jane Fonda), who's having an affair with his friend Jake (James Fox). Jake is the son of Val Rogers (E. G. Marshall), and Val is Mr Big around these parts. He's the bank manager and its owner, he builds the hospital, he appointed the sheriff (Brando). He doesn't know about Jake and Anna, but he knows that Jake doesn't like him ('Jake! Stop running away from me'). Then there are the two vice-presidents: Damon Fuller (Richard Bradford) and Edwin Stewart (Robert Duvall). Damon has curly grey hair, and he's smooth, man, smooth; he's having an affair with Edwin's trampy wife (Janice Rule), while his own (Martha Hyer) gets sodden with alcohol. It's the prissy Edwin who tells Val that Bubber has escaped, and that Anna is having an affair with his son. That triggers off the climax.

Bubber, meanwhile, has reached town and is hiding in a used-car lot. He sends his friend Lester (Joel Fluellen) with a message to Anna, but Lester is black, and when he's found lurking near her room, Damon and two equally drunken cronies want to lynch him. The sheriff takes Lester into jail for safe-keeping, while he waits for Jake and Anna to bring Bubber in for a fair hearing; but Val wants Jake back with him, and to get him he has to get from Lester where Bubber is. He tries to bribe him, and then beats him up – while Damon and buddies are beating up the sheriff. Val rushes to the dump, followed by Damon and cronies, the bloody sheriff and the whole town. Hooligans throw flames into the dump; someone spills a petrol-tank. The sheriff saves Bubber from the mob – but he's shot the next morning on the steps of the jail. The sheriff and his wife (Angie Dickenson) drive away to a new life, and, we trust, a more wholesome environment.

Movies about small-town corruption have been around since we were all in short trousers, but the trouble with this one is that it's small-minded; it lays blame all round (even on Bubber's mother, for making him what he is). It never suggests

Morituri, also known as *The Saboteur, Code Name Morituri*. Another of Brando's underrated films of the 60's

causes or reasons – but then, these movies never do. Val, the
man who can 'buy' everyone, is only pretending to be the
villain; as for Damon and his cronies, they're just small and
mean, hating niggers and beating up the sheriff. They're
drunk, too; and one of the best things about this movie is its
implicit picture of a boozy Saturday night. You'd have to go
back, coincidently, to *The Wild One*, for a like cinema portrait
of booze, boredom and heat.

Penn handles the glimpses of parties and bars well, and the
mob in action – the climax at the dump – is excitingly done; but
the film never comes to life. It's one of the three interesting
Brando films of the sixties, but it's a far cry, even, from *On the
Waterfront*. It's always a movie, looking like other movies;
you'd swear the town had been standing on the back-lot since
vacated by the Hardy family. The actresses are always that; and
there is a middle-aged couple (Henry Hull and Jocelyn
Brando) who walk the streets, commenting like a Greek
chorus, and they're ludicrous.

Then there's the script (no wonder Miss Hellman
repudiated it). The relationship of the father and son is so
hackneyed as to be laughable. *The Chase* offers a footling

analysis of the difficulties of the South, but once you're into lynching and like matters (the murder on the jail steps is even more serious) you can't without great skill remain within the conventions of melodrama. It might have been more convincing without the constant over-emphasis – of which the beating-up of the sheriff is the worst example. It's an unlikely happening, even if Damon and company hope the Big Man will protect them; and only in a movie could Brando be so blood-boltered and still walk.

He was not the first or last actor to make a speciality of screen suffering (Gary Cooper suffered severe rigours in most of his serious films of the fifties), but when it's as gratuitous as here some speculation is inevitable. As he's beaten to a pulp, you wonder whether he's not attempting allegory (not the least of which might be an actor's persecution by his following); it's difficult, otherwise, to understand what attracted him to the role. He's not too interesting in it (to be fair, most of the performance – which was mainly improvised – was left on the cutting-room floor: Penn has described that as 'marvellous'). It was as if he was marking time now that he had turned into middle-age, too old for heroes and rebels, too young for character parts – yet he has always been a character actor. This role could have been played by any no-longer-young star, by Wil-

The Chase: Brando as the small-town sheriff harassed by two of the townspeople

liam Holden or Gregory Peck, and he relies for the most part on the personality tricks which are their stock in trade. He does, however, make the sort of gestures they would never think of – examining at length the palm of his hand, running his pipe across his forehead; and he does in the end manage a portrait the way they never could – a prickly, awkward man, somewhat tainted by corruption (Rogers got him appointed) and uneasy about it. What integrity is left surfaces at the end, but meanwhile he's disenchanted not only with the town but with his wife. He's tired, a little dandyish, and given to violent outbursts. The film is packed with fine actors, and he dominates it.

American critics who hadn't seen through *Ship of Fools* (there are other examples, but why get depressed thinking of them?) saw through *The Chase*, and it did little better elsewhere. Brando realized that he needed a good film to regain his ascendency, for he shortened the odds, and for the next three years made two films a year – the first time he had worked as intensively since 1953. His second film in 1966 was *The Appaloosa*, and there is little to say about it.

It was made at Universal, and directed by Sidney J. Furie, a Canadian-born director who had arrived in Hollywood after a career in Britain and one big success (*The Ipcress File*). They didn't get on. Furie said: 'He's disorganized. No discipline at all. A procrastinator. One little scene that should have taken us a few hours to film took ten days. Every day he had another complaint – his tummy ached, his head ached – you should have heard the moans.' Brando's quarrels with Furie were the first indications of professional discord since *Mutiny* (he had got on notably well with Arthur Penn), and if it's of interest at all, it's because the film was a common or garden horse-opera, the sort of thing you'd imagine they'd saunter through. *Time* magazine made just that point: instead, their critic pointed out, 'Brando handicaps himself with a fiercely concentrated acting style more suitable for great occasions. He seems determined to play not just a man but a whole concept of humanity.'

Such ambitions have their rewards. Brando's brooding power brought something, an extra dimension to this tale of a loner set on revenge. With a Mexican accent and poncho, he played the Mexican-American who is constantly harassed and humiliated by a bandit general (John Saxon); when the bandit steals his horse – the appaloosa of the title – he sets out to even scores; at the climax, single-handedly, he takes on the whole gang. Even if there were echoes of earlier Brando films and performances, and even if this was, again, a role a fair number of Hollywood actors could play, he was able to create a tension which ran rings round his contemporaries. He was 'heavy' enough to fit into Mr Furie's grandiloquent designs, and into the beautifully photographed, autumnal, border country, in itself impressive enough to require a big actor for counterbalance.

The reviews were carping. The film had pretensions above its station, but the combination of Brando's presence and a strong plot made for a good entertainment movie – and Universal sold it that way. To most people it was just another movie, and the time for 'just another movie' was passing. The title wasn't helpful. In Britain they changed it to *South West to Sonora*, which was hardly more appealing. We were – for the first time in years – already anticipating his next film.

It promised to be a film *hors serie* – for it was written and directed by the one creative film-maker to whom few would deny the word genius: Charles Chaplin. Chaplin had left the United States in 1952, just after he had finished *Limelight*; he was persona non grata with the State Department, and, for equally foolish reasons, with most sections of the industry. He had made one film in the interim, in Britain, *A King in New York*, in 1957; it was made without the usual industry backing, and wasn't shown in the U.S. In 1966, the industry decided it was time to make up with Chaplin, and to atone for the years of neglect. Whether he approached Universal or whether Universal approached him isn't known; however, at that time Universal was involved in the production of films in Britain, and their British branch announced with pride that one of them would be the product of the world-famous and ageing prodigal son. He was being given as complete authority as he had enjoyed as his own boss, and carte blanche in the matter of the leading players.

In 1957, in an interview, when asked about contemporary actors, he said that he saw very few films, but he had seen Brando in *The Men*, and in one scene he had thought, 'this man has something'. The choice devolved upon Brando now because his ego demanded the biggest names around, regardless of who they were. Brando was the best actor in films, Sophia Loren was regarded as the most beautiful woman: both accepted without reading the script.

Filming did not go well. It began in an atmosphere of publicity and euphoria but when Brando began to perform under Chaplin's direction, he thought he was going 'raving mad': 'I was wanting to go to Charlie and say "I'm afraid we've made a horrible mistake".' He buckled under, and meekly took instructions, until he realized, perhaps, just how bad the film was going to be. In an effort to salvage something, he began to question some of Chaplin's commands, and shooting finished in hostile compromise. Chaplin later spoke disparagingly of him (though he made no reference to his inability to learn lines. Since *Mutiny on the Bounty*, at least, he had used cue cards, and later co-workers were to be further disconcerted by his habit of wearing earplugs on the set). The publicity was so intense that gossip about the differences between them was rife: but many a good movie had been forged in mutual dislike.

The film's opening, in London, in January 1967, amidst more publicity, continued its so-far triumphal progress in the world's press – till the truth was revealed in all its painful nakedness: the film was a bomb. The critics had only themselves to blame. Whatever Chaplin's powers as a young man, *Limelight* had been proof enough that they were failing – but you wouldn't have known it from reading the reviews. The Chaplin myth was upheld, through *A King in New York*, further, awful proof of a declining talent; and if the critics refused to reveal the truth, it is hardly likely that Chaplin was aware of it. But the industry is cautious: did any of Universal's executives take the trouble to see either film? – and if any of them read the script of this one, why didn't the share-holders sue for criminal negligence?

One might speculate – anything to postpone a discussion of the film itself. A sentence or two will suffice: we will console ourselves with Miss Loren's beauty, and let it return, hopefully, to oblivion. It was an old-fashioned comedy (originally thought-up by Chaplin in the late thirties for his then-wife, Paulette Goddard, and Gary Cooper) set in that playground of countless old movies, the ocean liner. Miss Loren was a White Russian countess of doubtful past who stows away in Brando's cabin; he was a wealthy diplomat who compassionately hides her, despite the fact that he has an important new ambassadorial post and is planning a reconciliation with his wife (Tippi Hedren). The dialogue was compounded of platitudes ('At this moment I'm very happy. That's all we can ask for') and archaisms ('You're just a common harlot'); wheezes included Miss Loren hiding in various cupboards and Brando scampering around without his trousers. There were jokes about seasickness and a rough-and-tumble climax in which Miss Loren, now loved by Brando, has to marry his compliant valet (Patrick Cargill). The stars caved in under the monotonous tread of the direction. Neither is a natural comedian, but Miss Loren was willing and high-spirited. Brando, having failed to find any humour in the script, played it straight; he's tried to give the man a character, or at least a distinctive way of walking, sitting, moving about, without finding any charm. Not surprisingly, they've both wilted long before the end of the picture, but they remain amiable towards each other and the audience. Their good will was not reciprocated.

At first the public refused to believe the critics. It was one of those films which starts the week well but is playing to empty houses by Saturday. Chaplin was incensed by the reviews, unprecedented in his long career, and he called the critics 'bloody idiots'. He was prevailed upon to cut twelve minutes (from 120 to 108 minutes, including almost all his own footage, in a cameo as an old steward), but it fared equally badly in New York.

11 OFF SCREEN; AND ONE VERY GOOD FILM

Two or three years earlier, Sophia Loren had talked of her first meeting with Brando: 'Shortly after I arrived in Hollywood Marlon Brando decided to introduce himself to me. He just walked into my dressing-room and prowled around, staring carefully at each of a number of original paintings which I had hung on the walls. After a long pause he turned and looked at me and sadly shook his head. "You're sick," he told me. "Emotionally disturbed." I asked him what made him think so. "Tell me," he said, "did you choose these paintings yourself?" "Yes, but what has that got to do with my being sick?" "Everything," Brando said. "The mere fact that you picked those particular ones clearly shows your state of mind. You know something? You're suffering. Deep down you have a secret emotional wound." "Well, never mind," I told him. "At least, I keep it secret. What a pity more people don't do the same." '

Brando's off-screen behaviour, ignored or overlooked during the late fifties, got more press coverage than his films in the years after *Mutiny on the Bounty*, soon revealed as the watershed of his career. He was just another movie-actor, involved with battles with his ex-wife over the custody of their child; involved in various romances which, to be sure, he didn't want publicized; involved with political and humanitarian causes in the name of Civil Rights. His conduct, in fact, made him an object of derision to what later became known as the Silent Majority, and a subject of interest or indifference to the more radically-minded.

The custody battles, and Brando's appearances in court, were clearly an embarrassment to him – as were interviews given by Miss Kashfi, and occasional articles by-lined by her, including 'Marlon Brando Is Out to Destroy Me – and He Will' (published in *Photoplay* at a time when he had temporary custody of the boy). In 1963 he went on the 'David Susskind Show' on television in an attempt to answer the riles of the gossip columns, and he said: 'I have two children growing up in this community and I think they deserve protection as do their mothers.' His second marriage had come to light in one of the custody trials of 1961 – a year earlier he had married Movita, who had played in the original *Mutiny on the Bounty*, and whom he had known since she had had a small role in *Viva Zapata!* There were two children, Michael and Rebecca,

Reflections in a Golden Eye: Brando and Elizabeth Taylor. The large picture of Brando is in the colours which Huston wanted to use for the film—but Warner's did not like his processed version, and released it only in Technicolor

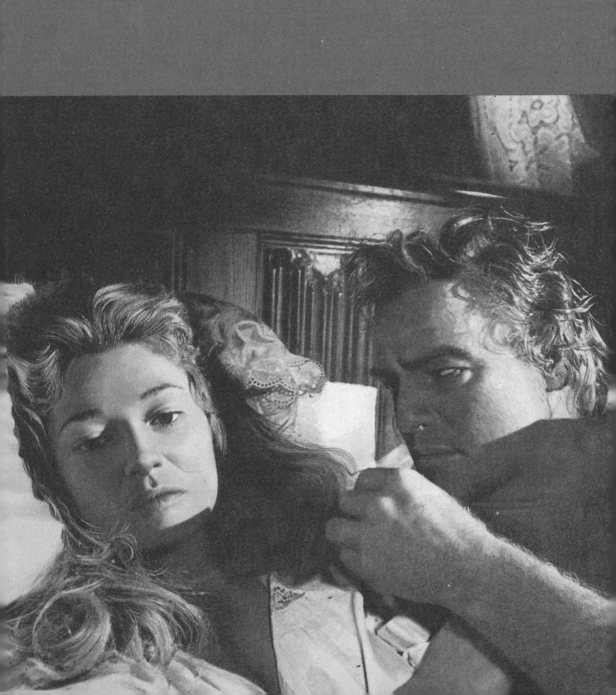

the second of which was born after they separated; when the marriage was annulled in 1968, Brando declared that neither child was his, which was strongly denied by their mother. As if he didn't have enough trouble publicly with the women he married, a Filipino dancer slapped a paternity suit on him in 1963. A blood test soon disposed of that, and Brando kept characteristically quiet about the rest of her revelations.

According to *Time* magazine, Brando is 'famous for his sometimes tumultuous off-screen romances', and from the same source comes this glimpse of the private Brando: 'What little is known of his true nature comes from a handful of his friends and associates. By their testimony, he is intelligent, warm, charming, compassionate, humorous and unpretentious, as well as undisciplined, boorish, gloomy, supercilious, cruel and downright bent. About the only thing everybody can agree on is that he is a prankster.' It is known that many of his affairs ended traumatically for the young ladies concerned, but with the exception of Miss Kashfi, none of them has so far made the details known to the press. In private life he is a tremendous mimic, and an amusing talker; his put-down of Miss Loren's paintings could be one of the deadpan jokes he enjoys. He can be disconcerting in conversation, when his sole object is to discover the real motives of the other speakers, and he is intensely quick to spot, and expose, phoneyness of any kind. His sympathy with the underdog led him into the Civil Rights movement, though some sources suggest that he is atoning for his fame, or the way he earns his money.

His interest in Civil Rights developed in the fifties, and in 1961 his signature appeared in an ad in *The New York Times* soliciting funds for Martin Luther King and the Struggle for Freedom in the South; other signatories included Eleanor Roosevelt, Harry Belafonte, Van Heflin, Nat King Cole and Elmer Rice. The text was sufficiently critical of police behaviour during a recent incident that the mayor of Montgomery, Alabama, tried to sue the paper for half-a-million dollars. He made appearances for the Civil Rights movement when he thought his presence might be useful, or just to add weight to other show business personalities equally incensed; and, one remembers too with some pride, he kept vigil outside San Quentin the night before Caryl Chessman was executed. (In 1960 Chessman had been sentenced to death for rape so long before, and had been so completely rehabilitated during the long years of his appeals, that his final sentence made no sense at all.) He was known to recommend black artists within the industry, and in 1964 hired a black secretary. That year he became interested in the plight of the American Indian, and, as with Civil Rights, gave financial help; and he spoke against apartheid in South Africa at the Central Hall in London. That was a public meeting, only partly full (his own appearance was unpublicized); Roy Moseley, who was with him, told me that

Left: *The Nightcomers:* Brando and Stephanie Beacham in a film based on some characters created originally by Henry James

backstage Brando was in tears contemplating how little he could actually do against that iniquitous cause.

There were fewer reports of film offers which came to nothing. In 1959, there was word that he would co-star with Sidney Poitier in *Paris Blues*, a story of white and black musicians in Paris, to be produced by Pennebaker. Pennebaker did make it, with Poitier, Paul Newman and Joanne Woodward. Brando, wisely, turned it down – on account of the script (as did Marilyn Monroe). He also refused the title-role in *Lawrence of Arabia*, offered while he was making *One-Eyed Jacks* – but then, he was probably offered first crack at every other major film role in the late fifties and early sixties.

All that had changed by 1967, although it was by no means his fault. At least two of his films had been unjustly handled by the press; *A Countess from Hong Kong* shouldn't have happened to anybody. The plum parts were now being offered to Paul Newman – ironically, for he had suffered earlier in his career from accusations that he imitated Brando (Newman was the first to admit that Brando was the superior actor, and he said that any film over which he had production control – e.g. *Butch Cassidy and the Sundance Kid* – was offered to Brando before any other actor). In 1967, the following at least were all considered bigger stars than Brando: Lee Marvin, Sidney Poitier, Steve McQueen, Dean Martin, Sean Connery, John Wayne, Richard Burton and James Coburn. Perhaps for the first time in his career, Brando found himself being

offered a role for which another actor had been contracted.

That actor was Montgomery Clift, then in such an advanced state of alcoholism as to be virtually unuseable; but his co-star was Elizabeth Taylor, and she wanted Clift. He died before filming began, and Miss Taylor (and Mr Burton as well) approved the substitution of Brando, who accepted second-billing for the first time since *A Streetcar Named Desire*. The film was *Reflections in a Golden Eye*, John Huston's version of the novel by Carson McCullers.

It opened in the U.S. six months after the Chaplin film, and failed just as totally. It opened in Britain another six months later, to an overwhelmingly favourable response from critics and public. Huston observed later: 'It's only now' – 1972 – 'beginning to become appreciated. More and more people . . . mention [it] as one of my better films. And I quite agree.' Maybe in the States its baroque quality seemed dated – and certainly the novel is faithfully followed in the screenplay by Chapman Mortimer and Gladys Hill. Both they and Huston have gone about their task in confident fashion.

The film begins (and ends) with a line from the first paragraph: 'There is a Fort in the South where some years ago a murder was committed.' Huston sketches in this army installation – the barracks, the captain's lecture room – and moves on to the married quarters, furnished in appropriate impersonal taste. It is a mellow, lingering autumn: sunlight dapples the woods where riders canter, and a soldier lurks in the

The final scene from the film, which is technically one of the most astonishing endings a film ever had bushes. One recalls that when Huston handled similar materials – *The Night of the Iguana* – he set his misfits just as firmly into their equally real and beautiful setting. Mrs McCullers used a plangent prose to deal with her subject, a muted quadrille for two army couples.

These are the Pendertons, Leonora (Miss Taylor), and Major Weldon Penderton (Brando). He is cold and prissy; she is uncomplicated, and she despises him. She is having an affair with Colonel Langdon (Brian Keith), whose sick wife, Alison (Julie Harris), is disliked by the three of them, living in a half-fantasy world with her Filipino houseboy, Anacleto. The soldier in the bushes, a Private Williams, has a crush on Leonora and takes to keeping vigil in her room at night, fingering her clothes; while, independently, the Major gets a fixation on him which at first he diagnoses as hatred. He follows him about, and when he sees him creep into the house, he thinks it is to visit him. He sits waiting, facing up to something he has been afraid to confront; and when the soldier goes past him to his wife's room, he takes a gun and shoots him dead.

The book delves only into the actions of these people, allowing but glimpses into their motives. They're set down, like flies in amber, basically pathetic. The things we remember most – that Alison has cut off her nipples with garden shears, that the Private rides 'bare-backed and bare-arsed' as Leonora puts it – are risible businesses for the cinema. Huston doesn't seem to have recognized the difficulties. The scene where Leonora whips her husband in front of the guests (which isn't in the book, and one might question its intrusion) works because he cuts at once to Anacleto gleefully reporting the details to Alison. He makes details tell – Alison's mute acceptance of the home to which she is committed, Leonora's boast that she can get away with murder because the C.O. dandled her on his knee as a baby. The film retains the gentle (and Jewish?) Captain Weincheck, who reads Proust and listens to music with Alison. Huston regards them all with non-maudlin compassion.

And he works in humour wherever possible: Leonora's trite, flighty remarks, the Major's pompous speech about the virtues of army life, 'a man's life among men'. It is the humour which saves the film as a film, which separates it from the book. The book is an elegant charade; the film draws on its fantasy for something more down-to-earth. It offers a more tangible army camp than did Mrs McCullers, and it poses its eccentrics more firmly in that world.

The focus inevitably shifts, offering three inter-related studies: the sick wife and her fawning houseboy; the illicit affair between the Colonel and the Major's wife; and a petty military man facing up to the fact that he's homosexual. And also, of course, the strange Private, but except for one telling, brief, scene in his barracks – where we learn that he doesn't 'relate' to his fellows – he is little more than an ikon.

With one exception, Huston has drawn extraordinary performances from his players. The exception, expectedly, is Miss Taylor, who pouts, primps and grimaces, and can't be stopped. In the book Leonora is stupid, but she's not vulgar. Miss Taylor *looks* vulgar, the huge breasts, the hair either piled high or tied back in a bandana, and it wouldn't matter if only she'd stop for a minute, but she's always busy. Apart from a certain voluptuousness she doesn't appear to have understood the character. Huston allows Zorro David (as Anacleto) to overdo things; he's not 'camp' in the book, but the humour is well-judged – and we see him through the Colonel's eyes. Brian Keith projects bemused virility, and it is only later – sodden drunk, or wanting Anacleto in the army to make a man out of him – that you realize he's as stupid as Major Penderton. As for Miss Harris, she comes closest to the character in the book.

Brando. This is the most difficult role. Mrs McCullers didn't understand how it is that an officer, in his forties, starts to lust after an enlisted man – though, via his fixation, she works well at it. The film makes a couple of mistakes: through a window, we watch the Major take out a postcard of a Greek male statue, and later he applies rejuvenating cream. These are jejune touches (though not out of character). Beyond the fact that it's repressed, we can only speculate about the Major's homosexuality; and Brando's is an astonishing study of sexual repression. It is the definitive study of the man beneath the uniform – practising with barbells, composing smiles in a mirror, revelling in his own tiny authority. In his own home, he is nothing; he manages to be curt with others, but his sexual frigidity, he suggests, well reaps the humiliation he accepts from his wife. He's a coward, he's self-important. After his horse has bolted, as he whips her his face is a vivid exposition of fury, of surprise, of affront – that the horse dared treat *him* so; it's the face of a spoilt child after his first spanking. Note also Brando's expression as he waits for the soldier – the tension one finds in Buñuel's shoe fetishists, the terror of an individual irrevocably committed to some sort of foolish or forbidden licentiousness. Both sequences are indicative of how much Brando dares – as he dares again in the 'English' accent he lays over the Major's Southern one. He manages, still, to lose words – which is why he's still accused of mannerisms – but you only have to see him set his head, his build and his facial muscles into the self-conscious stance of a little martinet, to realise how magnificent he can be when the conditions are right. Much thought went into this performance, and when you consider how badly it was received in his homeland, it's no wonder that he lost interest in his career – or so his next films would suggest.

12 FOUR FAILURES

Brando's salary for *Reflections in a Golden Eye* had been $750,000 plus 7½ per cent of the gross (it did not break even) – thus he had at least retained his fiscal position among movie stars. Julie Andrews, Sophia Loren, Miss Taylor and perhaps half-a-dozen others were said to be getting $1 million, but there was every indication that highly-paid stars were failing to attract the public. Some successful films were listed as flops because they didn't recover their costs – of which astronomical salaries were often a major part. In April 1968, *Variety* examined the recent track records of several well-paid stars and deduced that at least ten of them were not worth the salaries they were currently being paid. The ten included Glenn Ford, Tony Curtis, Yul Brynner, Rock Hudson, William Holden, James Garner, Anthony Quinn, Natalie Wood – and Brando. In each case, *Variety* looked at the total receipts of their last six films: in Brando's case these amounted to $9.6 million, or a paltry $1.6 million per film. *Variety* itself didn't draw the analogy, but the article was nearly as deadly as the exhibitors' infamous list of 'box-office poison' stars in 1938. Many of these names were 'saved' because the relation of star to film had changed, and many of the certified top-drawing stars were also turning out occasional flops. *Variety*'s inference was clear: these stars, and some others, had better reduce their salaries if they wanted to stay in business – and even then, they might not weather the storm. Brando probably would, the piece concluded, because he was regarded as '*the* American actor'.

No public announcement was made of his salary on his next two films, but the second was of obviously low-budget, and the other comprised what amounted to a guest appearance. As there were several other names in this project, and as he was instrumental in setting it up, it is probable that he worked for expenses and a percentage only. The film was *Candy*, adapted from a satire on pornography by Terry Southern and Mason Hoffenberg which had originally been published in France, in English, under a pseudonym. It became a cult book, an underground best-seller, and as the decade became more permissive it came out in the U.S. and Britain. The idea of filming it also originated in Europe, with Christian Marquand, an undistinguished French actor – and an old and close friend of Brando's. He wanted to direct, and when Brando agreed to appear in the film, Marquand had no difficulty in setting up a French–Italian co-production (though set in the U.S. it was filmed in Italy). Brando persuaded Richard Burton to play one of the other roles, about which time a Hollywood company – Selmur Pictures – became the third co-producer. Other names joined the cast – Walter Matthau, James Coburn, John Huston, Charles Aznavour, and the title-role was played by Ewa Aulin from Denmark, who at least looked okay as the naive teenager who wonderingly services several sex-starved men.

Left: *The Nightcomers:* Brando as the Irish groom

101

This was not – in 1968, at least – a likely subject for a film. The screenplay by Buck Henry altered the original, and was even more tasteless – except that words like 'tasteless' become meaningless in the context of *Candy*. It was meant to offend; it was meant to shock (there was a long sequence with blood splashing around a surgeon operating) and also to titillate. It was meant to amuse, but it had about as much wit as a hand-painted bedpan; it might have been assembled by a group of retarded and self-consciously daring adolescents. It diminished the reputation of all concerned, with the possible exception of Mr Matthau, who did his sequence with an expression of dour pessimism. Brando almost atoned for his back-stage role by twenty minutes of impeccable impersonation – which, unfortunately, came towards the end of the film, and thus the only reason to sit it through. Renata Adler in *The New York Times* summed him up: 'Marlon Brando, as a Jewish guru (the film has an ugly racialism and arrested development, frog-torturing soft sadism at its heart) is less unendurable, because one is glad to see him on the screen again.' The film itself reaped vile opinions, and after initial curiosity died at the box office.

The other film, *The Night of the Following Day*, was dismissed or disregarded; because of Brando, the critics regarded it on its initial dates, but it did little subsequent business and Universal opened it in most cities in the U.S. – and in Britain – as the lower half of a double-bill. It was not bad, and it's probable that its very lack of ambition had something to do with the way Universal sold it.

One of the executive producers was Elliott Kastner, whom Brando had known as one of his agents at M.C.A.; partnered with Jerry Gershwin, he was operating out of London. The producer and director was Hubert Cornfield, one of the industry's *maudit* talents (he had made *Pressure Point*, a low-budget but ambitious thriller; admired by some, execrated by others, it had failed financially and had not succeeded in getting him any subsequent work in films till this). Cornfield also wrote the script, with Robert Phipenny, from a novel by Lionel White. I do not know whether the novel was set in France, but the film offered no reason why these American crooks should be there, other than to provide an atmospheric setting – the marshes where they live, and the nearby, almost desolate, village. The teenage girl they kidnapped was played by Pamela Franklin; they were Brando, Rita Moreno as his wife, Richard Boone and Jess Hahn. There were intimations of emotional disturbance – the wife drugged herself, Boone was a sadist and child-molester – and the plot was carefully plotted till it fell into the crooks-fall-out formula and ended by being a dream. Brando, hair dyed blond as the brains of the gang, was accused by several critics of self-parody, and by others of having little seeming interest in the proceedings – charges

from which it would be difficult to exonerate him. He tried to get away from cliché by playing the ringleader as a man of moods, withal concerned for the girl's welfare, but it was his least rewarding work since he had entered films.

Before either film came out – *Candy* in late '68 and *The Night of the Following Day* in early '69 – it briefly seemed that relief was at hand: it was announced that Brando would star in *The Arrangement*, which Kazan would direct from his own novel. (Brando and Kazan had not seen each other for some years, but no matter.) However, after Martin Luther King was assassinated Brando announced that he had retired from the screen to devote his life to Civil Rights. Friends intimated that he   fered material likely to h   lm, an undistinguished o

or a film which would n   e's exploitation of the E   ontecorvo, best-known o   *a di Algeri*. Pontecorvo v   mmitted young Italian d   eally a good film, was c   e victims of Nazi con- c   we know as *The Battle* a   upulously fair account c   'rench out of Algeria. It v   aaking, for Pontecorvo, c   about where his own s

was by Franco Solinas a   octed by them and him (credits did not list an E   Brando agreed to do it, U   the film's three million dollar budget. There was talk of Sidney Poitier co-starring, but Pontecorvo thought his face too 'civilized' for the role of the black peasant leader, and he used an amateur, Evaristo Marques, discovered in Colombia, where the locations were to be shot. They were begun in Cartegena, in uncomfortable heat, and with, in Pontecorvo's own words, 'thousands of extras who had never seen a camera before. Marlon was not helped by this atmosphere of noise and confusion which obviously affected his nerves (he wears wax earplugs on the set and can't bear to catch an eye-line behind the camera). But this was the price we had to pay for shooting the film live . . .'

Brando and Pontecorvo did not get on; Brando called him a dictator, and objected to endless takes, perhaps because he wasn't calling the shots: 'If he wants a purple smile from me and I give him a mauve smile, he continues ordering me to smile until he gets exactly what he wants.' Pontecorvo later spoke about him: 'I think Brando has a somewhat difficult character and would have had the same problems with any European director – indeed, I gather he did with Chaplin. American actors are accustomed to a freedom that the more *engage* European directors cannot concede to their actors. American film actors are spoilt. Just because they are often good they think it gives them the right to interfere where no one has asked them to interfere. The idea that a European director has of his film is his alone . . .'

The quarrels became bitter enough for Brando to refuse to continue shooting in Colombia; the producer, Alberto Grimaldi, had the unit transferred at great cost to Morocco, where filming finished. Its troubles were not over: the Spanish government objected to the title, *Quemada*, which suggested that the colonial system indicated was Spanish – so the Portuguese version of the word was used, *Queimada!* In the U.S. it was called *Burn!*, but few people heard of it under any title; when it opened there at the end of 1970, twenty minutes had been shorn from the footage, but that was only one reason for the depressed state of the undertaking. Pontecorvo's expressed aim was to combine action and polemic, which he had done, flawlessly, with *The Battle of Algiers*; this was a ham-fisted effort.

Brando was Sir William Walker, an English gentleman sent to Queimada, a Portuguese colony (so-called – Queimada means Burn – because fire was once used to quell a native rebellion); his mission was to ferment revolt among the natives because the British government wanted an end to Portuguese monopoly in the sugar trade. He chooses a dockside porter, José Dolores (Marquez), for his foil, by provoking him and then involving him in a robbery. The robbery forces Dolores to kill Portuguese soldiers – and become an enemy of the State; after which it is not difficult for Sir William to persuade him to gather other disaffected portions of the black population about him and lead them in revolt. At the same time, Sir William works his wiles on a liberal, Sanchez (Renato Salvatori), persuading him that it is his Christian duty to assassinate the governor. Dolores assumes the leadership of the country, but after his rebel army and ineffectual government have brought the country to ruin, he's persuaded to resign and Sanchez becomes governor. Sir William leaves for home. Ten years later he's sought out, this time by the British Royal Sugar Company: Dolores, still living by the revolutionary precepts taught him by Sir William, is continuing to create unrest, and he is hired to bring the country back to peace – that is, commercial prosperity. The country is now a republic, and Sanchez is still governor. When he realizes that he is a pawn of British commercial interests, Sir William manoeuvres a plot to unseat him and has him shot. The British agents combine with the corrupt Portuguese officials and their black army to rout out Dolores: Sir William gives him a chance to escape but he prefers to die a martyr. Sir William prepares to depart, his job done; on the quayside he is approached by another dock-porter, who stabs him.

As a tract, the piece is, if not original, at least ambitious, though you might pertinently ask what the Italian writers and director know about British or Portuguese colonialism in the late eighteenth century? (In fact, its flailing aim is indicated by some origins: secret government intervention on behalf of

Overleaf: Gillo Pontecorvo's *Queimada !*, also known as *Burn*. Brando as the English emissary with Evaristo Marquez and (inset) Renato Salvatore

sugar interests is characteristic of the American colonialization of Hawaii, and the rest of the plot mirrors events in French Hawaii.) They may feel deeply about the indecencies and abuses of the colonial system, and their indignation is just – except that this film always seems like an *exercise* in indignation. We know about corruption, about heroes becoming martyrs, about petty tyrants – they're old screen material (much of this is *Viva Zapata!*, with Dolores as Zapata, Sir William as Fernando): the best of this movie is when it gets closest to history to show how commercial interests were allowed to predominate. Sir William is woefully misconceived: first he's on this side, then on that, a spokesman for both the British government and the natives, a man caught between his job, his own guile, and a lingering idealism. Outside his role as spokesman, the little we learn of him, and it's after the ten year gap, is that he's been blackballed from his club; a real fallen hero, he's found fighting in a low pub. Brando plays with the same accent he used in *Mutiny on the Bounty*, but little else – he never seems to get the measure of him. There is some play made over his confrontation with Dolores – a love-hate relationship or something similar, but it goes for nothing. It was courageous of him to take on the role; perhaps with closer co-operation between actor and director, there might have been more cohesion.

At the same time, it fails as an action movie. In the old days, with a film thus full of inconsistencies, of plot-angles dropped, of irresolute changes of mood or tempo, the thing to do was to make it move so fast that the audience didn't notice: but Pontecorvo lingers, with native marches, scenes of revelry and butchery. They're prettily photographed, but fatal to the film's impact. There's a nice feeling for the ambience of equatorial islands, and why not?

With the failure of *Queimada!*, Brando's professional life reached its lowest level, a depth undreamt of in the palmy days. The life of an actor cannot be all roses – at various times, Clark Gable, Gary Cooper, James Cagney and Cary Grant were considered washed-up; Charles Laughton had spent years in silly films in roles unworthy of him – as, around this time, were Trevor Howard and James Mason. A decline in popularity is almost inevitable with ageing (it is happening at last, as I write, to John Wayne), but Brando was a comparatively young man – he was only 46. We thought he could have gone to the moon, or as Rod Steiger put it more realistically: 'He could have done anything, *anything*, however difficult or uncommercial, on the screen and taken the critics, the industry, the fans with him. But he didn't choose to. I don't know why.'

He did choose to: *Queimada!* could be termed 'difficult and uncommercial', but even in its final faulty state it was more interesting than most films. He chose with consistency what he hoped were solid entertainment movies with some message and a good, not too showy, role for himself. Of his failures, only two were out-and-out bad movies, *A Countess from Hong Kong* and *Candy*. *The Chase* and *Queimada!* were both of two seemingly doomed breeds: the former a demonstration of the pitfalls lying in wait for earnest talents tackling social injustice within the Hollywood system, the latter the latest of a series of imbroglios involving European creative talent and American stars and American money. Only *The Night of the Following Day* was a pot-boiler. *Morituri* and *The Appaloosa* were entertainments unfairly dismissed; the reception accorded *Reflections in a Golden Eye* in the U.S. is a matter for pathologists. Some critics continued to take Brando seriously; it was the lesser ones who slapped him down, like teachers reprimanding the brightest boy in the class because he'd become swollen-headed or wasn't trying hard enough. The fans remained curious about his work even when they didn't bother to go and see his films. Steiger had become a bigger star than Brando, reckoned more bankable by the industry; George C. Scott, like Steiger, hadn't the Brando asset of film-star looks, but he also was more in demand. James Mason observed that Scott was probably the No 1 star in the U.S. 'now that Brando has presumably conceded and retired. Brando has made such a balls-up of his career.'

Certainly, after *Queimada!* Brando chose badly – perhaps out of desperation. He accepted a script sent him by a young British director, Michael Winner, but even with his acceptance Winner was turned down by, in his own words, 'every American company and every British company'. Winner eventually did get backing, with the connivance of three American producers working in Britain, Elliott Kastner again, Jay Kanter and Alan Ladd Jr; he and Brando took no salary, anticipating the eventual profits. After almost a year on the shelf and a screening at the 1971 Venice film festival, it was bought by Avco-Embassy for $650,000, and then, probably, only because Brando's 'comeback' in *The Godfather* was expected to restore him to his former glory.

At all events, Winner's acquisition of Brando was a coup. In ten years of making features his most notable qualities had been persistence and a gift for self-publicity, neither of which disguised the fact that none of his films was of a quality to suggest why an actor even of Brando's reduced calibre should want to work with him; while he himself was disliked by almost everyone who had ever worked with him. With Brando, he did not feel his customary compulsion to be rude, and they got on: as he put it, 'a director must be chameleon-like . . . Marlon Brando likes a lot of jokes on the set, surprisingly. He's delighted to be gagging around . . . able to perform quite seriously a few seconds after being involved in hilarious humour . . .'

The film concerned, *The Nightcomers*, was, unfortunately,
no joke. It was based on the sort of conceit usually found on the
B.B.C.'s Third Programme or in the Christmas competition
pages of the weeklies. Michael Hastings wrote it; an investiga-
tion into the proceedings at Bly House before Miss Giddens
arrives – an extension of 'The Turn of the Screw' (filmed
almost a decade earlier, as *The Innocents*). It was a prologue
posing as the thing itself, a six-minute event dragged out to
ninety-six.

The guardian (Harry Andrews), is disinterested in both the
house and the children, leaving them to the care of the housekeeper, Mrs Grose (Thora Hird), the governess, Miss Jessel
(Stephanie Beachum), and the valet-cum-handyman, Peter
Quilp (Brando). Quilp is an untidy, drunken, Irish yarn-
spinner, and the children, with nothing else to do, are
influenced by his shabby, nihilistic view of the universe; and
their outlook on life is further perverted when Miles spies on
Quilp and Miss Jessel at their love-making– consisting mainly
of what the small-ads call 'bondage'. The children begin to
taunt and persecute Mrs Grose; and when Miss Jessel tires of
Quilp and plans to leave they murder her. Miles confesses the
crime to Quilp before shooting him with an arrow.

Apart from the impertinent assault on the ethics of Henry
James (can you imagine him so graphically chronicling these
sado-masochistic sex-games?) the film doesn't have a mod-
icum of understanding about English country-house life
seventy years ago. Even if 'bullshit' was a common epithet
then, it's unlikely that even the uncouth Quilp would use it
before a lady, even his mistress in bed; it's even more unlikely
he'd say 'fart' before children. Even if this Quilp is a self-
confessed rebel (is that what attracted Brando to the role?), his
conduct is idiotic. He would never have been kept on by
guardian or housekeeper – tieless and long-haired, he even
turns up at the funeral of the children's parents dressed like a
tramp. Photographs of the period give a lie to all this: he might
have found employment as a corporation dustman, but never
as a groom (let alone a valet).

Brando's performance was like the film– without bite, without point, without atmosphere (the film was prettily photographed in cold winter sunlight, but is never so sinister as the
summer gardens were in *The Innocents*). He seems to have
been influenced by his work in *The Wild One*, where he also
played a misfit and a layabout, but– at least– in that film it was
fascinating to watch him work through his inarticulateness to
express his thoughts. Here, he varies between loquaciousness
and moody silences. As in *Last Tango in Paris*, later, he
seemed bored by everything, even the bed-antics. Still, Winner
says the film gave him 'far and away the most personal satisfac-
tion in recent years'. He doesn't say whether Avco-Embassy
got back much of their money.

T he Godfather saved Brando's bacon; and it brought him back to the sort of superior Hollywood product in which he had made his name (though he is thought to have turned down the role of Rasputin in *Nicholas and Alexandra*). It was also his first work in the U.S. since *The Appaloosa*; (apart from some locations, *Reflections in a Golden Eye* was made in Italy). He had maintained a house in Beverly Hills (it had once belonged to Howard Hughes, and was appropriately guarded like Fort Knox), and though for a time in the late fifties he did appear at Hollywood premieres and parties, he did not for long live the high life; he now spent most of his time in Tahiti, with which he had fallen in love during the making of *Mutiny on the Bounty*. His romantic interest in that film, Tarita, is his wife there under local law, and they have two children. She gave up films because he asked her to, but after the birth of their daughter, Tarita-Cheyenne, in 1970, she complained of neglect and went to live in Paris. He asked her to come back, and the boy, Teihotu, was born in 1971. He had bought an island, Tetiarora (in fact, an atoll of thirteen islands), about thirty miles north of Tahiti itself, where he raises lobsters and studies marine ecology, reads books on Eastern philosophy and politics, and lives, so it appears, in perfect contentment – except for uninvited journalists who, naively, do not understand why he considers them intrusive. He is not Joan Crawford. 'Privacy is not something that I'm merely entitled to' he once said, 'it's an absolute prerequisite.' Attempts to see him were to multiply with the success of his two next films – though he did grant interviews during the making of *The Godfather*, for which privilege, it was reported, Paramount paid him $100,000.

Left: Trauma in a flat in Passy in *Last Tango in Paris* —Brando and Maria Schneider

The story of the filming of *The Godfather* was itself news. Paramount had been offered it as a script by Mario Puzo, an unsuccessful novelist; they told him to turn it into a novel, and they'd finance him the while. The novel became a best-seller, having got some good notices – and if I may digress for a moment, after the film came out, its publisher wrote to *Variety* complaining that every reviewer had referred back to the novel and described it as trashy. I checked a piece I had written on the film before seeing it: I had called the book 'meretricious', and I'll stick. It was sensationalist and both over- and ill-written. It did give a vivid picture of an incredible kind of private enterprise, where men lived dangerously, unsure of their friends and expecting imminent death.

Paramount assigned Albert Ruddy to produce, but it was Robert Evans, the head of production, who chose the director, Francis Ford Coppola, regarded in the industry as a failure – partly because his three films had not performed up to expectations (though no one seeing them – *You're a Big Boy Now*, *Finian's Rainbow* and *The Rain People* – could doubt that he was an imposing talent). Brando wanted to play the title-role:

113

Paramount weren't remotely interested. He offered to test, or, rather, did an impromptu test at home. Coppola wanted him, and Paramount grudgingly submitted: Brando stated that his fee was $250,000 plus a percentage, but *Variety* reported that it was for a percentage only. Filming was unhappy at first, though Coppola says that Brando was a tower of strength to cast and crew. The trouble was between him and the Front Office, and at one point they sought to replace him with Kazan, on the thesis that only Kazan could handle Brando. But Coppola hung on: 'The things they were going to fire me over were, one: wanting to cast Brando. Two: wanting to cast [Al] Pacino. Wanting to shoot it in period. The very things that made it different from any other film.' He was, of course, proved right, and he should also be praised for his work on the script: though credited to both him and Puzo, it was much superior to the book – the junk had gone, the Harold Robbins stuff. What's left was a vivid picture of an incredible kind of private enterprise, etc.

The problem of handling a vast and teaming subject was solved by concentrating on the main handful of characters and letting the rest dangle (a method adopted in another current movie, from another best-seller, a very different one, *Nicholas and Alexandra*). Gone was the dreary business of the marital problems of the Hollywood star, Johnny Fontanne, though he was retained – presumably to stress the fact that the Godfather's power spread to Hollywood. With the exception of Kay Adams (Diane Keaton), the nice non-Italian girl who falls in love with Michael (Pacino), none of the women matter at all – and the reaction of her family to her marrying a Mafia man is barely touched on. She serves a plot function; as does the Corleone girl who marries the thuggish husband – because he'll be the decoy to lead to the death of Sonny (James Caan). Mother (Morgana King) is but glimpsed: her grief when the Godfather is wounded is of no account.

And so it goes. Other gang-leaders appear to be consulted or to be threatened, and in both instances to be gunned down. The corrupt police chief (Sterling Hayden) is murdered by Michael after that memorable meal in Brooklyn. The family cohorts, including Hagen (Robert Duvall), the consigliore or lawyer, do little more than dance attendance on the Godfather and the two sons who matter. The casting is perfect: the few familiar faces and the many unfamiliar ones. Pacino grows from callow kid to the new leader; Caan is cheery as the extrovert Sunny. Brando manages to look like an old man. His gestures are slow, his hands eloquent in a lordly, elderly-Italian manner. He looks at people the way old men of power look at people, inquisitively, graciously. He smiles mirthlessly, and talks in a hushed, authoritative voice, and the authority remains when he's off-screen. It's a construction job rather than a performance, but there's no strain and nothing jars – which is rare when actors play character roles older than their years.

Whether it was worth his trouble (other than in restoring his prestige, in commercial terms) is something else again. Both he and Coppola said they saw the story as a metaphor for the U.S. Violence, and organized violence is, as we're often told, part of the American way of life. Everything in the movie is true – Coppola, for instance, feels that no previous film had managed to paint an honest picture of Italian–American families, but this particular family is not typical and the film – like the book – is finally ambivalent about their trade. There's no message and no moral: the family will go on with a new leader, and society will continue to look away or, at best, compromise.

Coppola intended no more. This is a film of tremendous accomplishment. The Sicilian scenes escape the patronizing tone of most American films about Italy, the period detail is remarkable – but despite the incidentals, despite the skill and the transparent honesty, *Scarface*, at half the length, is more exciting. And it's far less likeable than either *Gone With the Wind* or *The Sound of Music*, both of which it surpassed as the most financially successful film of all time, as the saying goes.

Before it was premiered, however – in March 1972 – Brando had begun another film which would be as much – if not more – discussed: *Last Tango in Paris*, or, to give it its correct title(s) – for it was a French–Italian co-production with only minimal American backing, *Dernier Tango à Paris* or *Ultimo Tango in Parigi*. His salary was $200,000 plus the inevitable percentage. It was a further flirtation with the European cinema, and the director was Bernardo Bertolucci, then riding a crest after *Il Conformista*. With him and Brando, the press office of United Artists (handling the French end of the production, and world-wide distribution) knew they had something. When it was let out that the movie had a high sex content, the presses of the world throbbed with anticipation.

The film was invited, and sent, to the 1972 New York film festival, in the hope that favourable American reviews would avert the expected censorship problems in Italy; and an apparently eminent American critic, Pauline Kael, wrote a notice (in *The New Yorker*, which, parenthetically, once had a reputation for the concinnity of its writers) in which she claimed that the film was as important an event in the history of the arts as the first night of 'The Rite of Spring' in 1913. *Time* magazine did a cover story entitled 'Love and Death in Paris', and there were whispers about sodomy as well as speculation on the film's involvement with art and censorship (invoking memories of *A Streetcar Named Desire*). It opened in Paris, it opened in New York; it opened in London, shorn of the scene where Brando sodomizes the girl with his trousers on – by which time, the presses of the world had ensured that

Overleaf: Again *The Last Tango in Paris*: Brando in the infamous flat, but the girl this time is Catherine Allegret

there wasn't a literate person in the world who hadn't heard of it. As it opened, United Artists were predicting that it would overtake *The Godfather* as the most successful film ever made.

You might consider what it was the public would find more enticing than Vivien Leigh loving Clark Gable, Julie Andrews carolling in the hills above Salzburg or the carnage of the Mafia: a melancholy anecdote about an American widower in Paris and the girl he picks up in an empty apartment. They are both looking for a flat; he (Brando) is mourning his wife, she (Maria Schneider) is about to marry a young movie director (Jean-Pierre Léaud). He is sulky and rude; she is bright, casual, unruffable. After the publicity, it is no surprise to find that he has pinned her against the wall within seconds and is unbuttoning his fly – uncomfortable and unlikely, but not, in the circumstances, entirely incredible. He proposes that they continue to meet for that purpose – no ties, no surnames, just sex for the hell or the fun of it. Given the hangdog expression adopted by Brando since the first frame, it is hardly surprising that this is his scene or wherever the action now is in Paris. More seriously, he is a man going downhill, expended, a man beaten-up by life and betrayed; he wants no commitment beyond the sexual one, but he finds, only too soon, that it isn't enough. He talks about his past and encourages her to talk about her life. In the end, when she tells him that her marriage is imminent, he follows her, pleading, 'You know you're a jerk. The best fucking you'll ever get is right here in this apartment.' He follows her home, and she takes out a gun and kills him – always a good way to end a movie which has run out of steam (this sort of 'stop' to a movie, a common let-out in several rotten films of the sixties and seventies, was considered indecent by earlier film-makers – see Frank Capra's memoir). Dilys Powell wrote in *The Sunday Times*: 'Bertolucci has been reported as making the usual glib pronouncements about the impossibility people "in our society" find in communicating with another. His idea, then, was to show two figures in isolation who communicate solely through sex.' Death, of course, is the final isolation, with death there is no further communication; but for a film-maker of any aspiration it's a cop-out.

This movie certainly raises doubts about Bertolucci's talent; it is altogether quieter and less glittering tha *Il Conformista* and the other films which preceded it, but when it does liven up it is only too reminiscent of their virtuoso passages. We are relieved of the room in Passy quite early, via some glossy flashbacks; later, when Brando returns to his home, it turns out to be a flophouse (there's no reason why it shouldn't be, but no reason why it should be, either). We learn that his wife had a lover (Massimo Girotti), there are clients knocking to be let in. When one client deserts his whore, Brando tears

after him for a spot of beating-up against modernists billboards (close-ups of billboards being de rigueur in all sub-Godard movies). The last tango itself takes place on a dance-floor eerily like that in *Il Conformista*, with Brando and the girl drunk on champagne, shocking the patrons as the lesbian dance shocked us in the earlier film.

At this point, Brando unlooses his trousers and exposes his behind to a patron – a practice called 'mooning', and indulged in as a joke, so went the publicity, on the set of *The Godfather* by Brando and other cast members. The practice suggests an infantilism hitherto unsuspected in a profession not noted for maturity, but the fact that it turns up here confirms a suspicion that Brando is the real *auteur* of *Last Tango*. Bertolucci said that they discussed each scene before shooting, in perfect accord, but the extent of Brando's participation can be gauged by another remark of Bertolucci's, that the film is 'a melange of Hollywood and European cinema', which it isn't at all: there's nothing of Hollywood in it. He also said that he 'decided that to suggest and allude instead of saying it outright would create an unhealthy climate for the spectator' – but the sex isn't explicit (the girl is seen nude, but Brando only in part and discreetly). These are the expected, bourgeois remarks from this *Italian* director: what he shows may be shocking to him (his earlier films reveal no exhibitionist desires in the manner of Vadim or Ken Russell). Brando, he admitted, improvised (no cue cards!) much of the dialogue of *Last Tango*, including the reminiscences of his youth – dialogue which has all the scintillation and wit of the monologues in lesser Godard or the exchanges in 'The Changing Room'. As David Leitch wrote in *The New Statesman* (under a review headed '*Merde de Taureau*'): 'Brando's ad-libbing, dredged from that area of Hemingway the novelist was too rigorous to publish, speaks for itself. An amazingly deft amalgam of the worst of "To Have and Have Not" and "Across the River and Into the Trees".'

The dialogue of the 'love' scenes is, at least, of a new cinema level. 'What strong arms you have' she says. 'The better to squeeze a fart out of you' he replies, going on with the Red Riding Hood analogies to talk of crabs and putting his tongue in her rear. Later, she: 'What are we doing in this apartment?' He: 'Let's just say we're taking a flying fuck at a doughnut' – and that's the nearest this film gets to a glimmer of humour. As for the sodomy, him with his trousers on, using butter as a lubricant, you wonder that grown people can offer it as entertainment, or a comment on human behaviour or whatever. It is supposed to represent the degradation to which the girl has sunk, after which she must reassert sanity and return to her film director – but *Screw* magazine and *Playboy* would have us believe that it's common practice among 'liberated' couples; and, anyway, Brando degrades her even more heinously in his tirade – wanting to see her fucked by a pig, etc. He then goes home to look at his wife's corpse, abusing her in the same manner for about five minutes. The two scenes together make up the most repellently misogynist sequence of any movie yet made.

There has been much speculation – in *Time* and elsewhere – as to what extent Brando improvised the 'love'-making; as to how much it is his scene. It is hard to imagine this hitherto prudish director insisting on it – hard to imagine the scenes with Jean-Louis Trintignant and Dominique Sanda, his original choices for the roles. It is not hard to imagine the otherwise private Brando, a masochist in several previous movies, deciding on a sort of Christ-like atonement for being a film star; he succeeds in holding his dignity, because of the sad lion's head and the uncanny way he has imagined himself into this gruesome, middle-aged failure – the most direct playing of a derelict by any Hollywood actor that the screen has known. (It is curious: Miss Schneider says, 'As he thinks himself old, only one thing interests him – his make-up. He is lazy, indolent . . . and he drinks too much. Only one thing interests him – love.') It is Bertolucci who becomes suspect. We do not know which of them made the new-to-them discovery that people play games during sex, but after a self-conscious display by Brando and Schneider it is Bertolucci, obviously, who cuts to a shot of two ducks – an unnecessary introduction to scenes of Leaud filming, and a very clumsy device.

The film abounds in such devices – like the razor Brando fondles – he may have a death wish, but it's a hack-movie way of creating tension. Bertolucci's central idea, the sexual congress with a stranger is a release from loneliness, is not new, but it's new for films (or almost: in *Mademoiselle*, directed by Tony Richardson and written by Jean Genet, an unbalanced schoolmistress and an Italian immigrant woodcutter come together from loneliness, and they too bay like dogs as a prelude to love-making; Brando had toyed with this script some seven years earlier before relinquishing it). It could still make a good movie – there is strength in this room, and these two characters (and as played by these two); but it would have to be in either French or in English and not in this uneasy mixture. Anyone who has lived in Paris knows how easily bilingual French and Americans slip from one language to the other, but in this movie it's show-off, quite unnatural, as if United Artists wanted both an art movie and a commercial one – hedging their bets, the best of all possible worlds, etc. What *is* here is inescapably dreary: two hours nine minutes of what might have been a footnote in Kraft-Ebbing.

The public sensed this; within a few month's of the film's opening, United Artists revised their estimates of its eventual earnings. It is unlikely, now, that its final take will be vertiginous. Its reputation as the most 'candid' major film yet made – outside the more consciously cheery soft- and hard-core por-

118

nographic movies – was offset by the fact that no one who saw it considered it erotic; but that was offset again by the fact that it was mentioned in all the arguments and battles waged over censorship in 1973 (and, in fact, it was banned in occasional backward towns).

There was another reason to discuss Brando in the spring of 1973. *The Godfather* brought him a slew of awards, despite the fact that his antics in *Last Tango* had alienated the industry more completely than his lack of drawing-power a year earlier. He refused the Hollywood foreign correspondents' Golden Globe Award. He was nominated for an Oscar, and won, but he did not turn up to collect it. Instead, an unknown Indian girl, Sasheen Littlefeather, was catapulted into world fame by turning up at the Awards ceremony to read a speech by him as to why he was refusing it. The audience began to boo, and she didn't finish it, but Brando had got publicity for the cause nearest to his heart – the plight of the Indian in present-day America. He later sent a copy of the speech to *The New York Times* and other papers, and it was admirably argued, if a bit naive in the belief that he was punishing the Academy or the industry for the treatment meted out to the American Indian by movies since their inception.

The publicity was entirely adverse: he had used Hollywood's gala night for politicizing; he had been too cowardly to come in person, and, worse, hid behind a woman's skirts; and Gregory Peck's comment was not entirely uncalled-for, that if Brando wanted to make a gesture he might have offered the Indians some of his enormous earnings from *The Godfather* and *Last Tango*. What was uncomfortably clear, however, was that his rejection of the award was entirely consistent with the worst of his public behaviour since he first achieved fame: he was showing off in the worst sort of megalomaniac film-star way. He acted in the way most convenient to him, typically misunderstanding the actual importance of the Oscar ceremonies: if the cause was really dear to him, he could have gone on every talk-show in the U.S. to air his views. This was pointed out to him, and he accepted an invitation to appear on Dick Cavett's show in July, when he talked about the Indian cause with, said *Variety*, 'conviction and indignation'.

He said that his next film would be about the cause, and he turned down the sequel to *The Godfather*, or, rather, he said he would only do it for a ridiculously high price – $500,000 plus 10 per cent of the profits, said *Variety*, for what was merely a cameo role. Paramount declined to meet his price. Since then, the only other *reports* of acting offers have been from Italy, but, for the record, one should note that just before *Last Tango* he signed for *Child's Play*, but left the cast after differences with the producer, David Merrick (Robert Preston played his role). *Last Tango* and the Oscar business had undone much of the good done by *The Godfather*, and the industry continued to evolve, moving away from the prima donnas and the legends. He was no longer the industry's rebel, but a pariah, an outsider; no longer the golden boy, but a chubby middle-aged man with a gaunt-face and grey locks falling to his shoulders. He spoke of retiring, and terminated his contract with his agent, saying that he doubted whether he'd need him again. His indifference to his career had probably been increased by his last two films, which had restored him to glory and a seemingly limitless earning capacity (on September 4th, 1973 *Variety* reported that Brando had pocketed $1,600,000 of his 'cut-off' profits from *The Godfather*, and that his agent was estimating that he would earn $3 million from *Last Tango*). Besides, after stuffing your cheeks with cotton-wool for the highest-earning film ever made, and baring your soul for the most-discussed movie in a decade, what is there left to do? Maybe it has something to do with the way he looked in *Last Tango*, or the effect of the whole depressing enterprise, but one is tempted to see him as a spent force. Olivier remains thought-of as the world's best actor, not because he once played the classics, and superbly, but because he has gone on doing so, gone on accepting the challenges open to a leading actor, well past middle-age. As England's greatest actor, he is loved within the industry and without, and has climaxed his career by heading Britain's National Theatre. But America's greatest actor, having achieved some sort of notoriety for sodomising a girl with his trousers on, remains, more sadly, a matter of doubt and distrust to many of his fellow-countrymen. Whatever it is that spurs an actor on – money, the need for affection, the need for display, ambition, power, creativity – it could hardly be for this.

In retrospect, his achievements may be more admired; he may have more to offer. He said in 1972 that he no longer despised acting, but sometimes the effort seemed too great: 'You have to upset yourself. Unless you do, you cannot act. And there comes a time when you don't want to anymore. You know a scene is coming where you'll have to cry and scream and all those things, and you can't just walk through it; it would be really disrespectful not to try to do your best.'

He can still be stirred. Edward Albert, the actor (he lived near Brando in Tahiti for a while in 1970) suspects that 'he believes somewhere along the line he missed something he could have done, something he could have been. It's as if somebody had put an angel inside of him, and he's aware of it; and,' he added, 'it's more than he can contain.'

The last of Brando ?—
Last Tango in Paris—
Brando and Maria
Schneider

Filmography

1950 The Men
Stanley Kramer Productions–United Artists. Director: Fred Zinnemann. Producer: Stanley Kramer. Story and screenplay by Carl Foreman. Music: Dimitri Tiomkin. Photographed by Robert de Grasse. 85 minutes. New York premiere: July. With Marlon Brando (Ken), Teresa Wright (Ellen), Everett Sloan (Dr Brock), Jack Webb (Norm), Richard Erdman (Leo), Arthur Jurado (Angel), Virginia Farmer (Nurse Robbins), Dorothy Tree (Ellen's mother), Howard St John (Ellen's father), Nita Hunter (Dolores).

1951 A Streetcar Named Desire
Charles K. Feldman Group Productions–Warner Bros. (When Feldman's agreement with Warners expired, distribution was taken over by 20th Century-Fox.) Director: Elia Kazan. Producer: Charles K. Feldman. Screenplay by Tennessee Williams, from his own play, adapted by Oscar Saul. Music: Alex North. Photographed by Harry Stradling. 122 minutes. New York premiere: September. With Vivien Leigh (Blanche du Bois), Marlon Brando (Stanley Kowalski), Kim Hunter (Stella), Karl Malden (Mitch), Rudy Bond (Steve Hubbell), Nick Dennis (Pablo Gonzales), Peg Hillias (Eunice Hubbell), Wright King (the young collector).

1952 Viva Zapata!
20th Century-Fox. Director: Elia Kazan. Producer: Darryl F. Zanuck. Screenplay by John Steinbeck, from *Zapata the Unconquered* by Edgcumb Pichon. Music: Alex North. Photographed by Joe MacDonald. 113 minutes. New York premiere: February. With Marlon Brando (Emiliano Zapata), Jean Peters (Josefa Espejo), Anthony Quinn (Eufemio Zapata), Joseph Wiseman (Fernando Aguirre), Arnold Moss (Don Nacio), Lou Gilbert (Pablo), Alan Reed (Pancho Villa), Margo (Posadera), Harold Gordon (Don Francisco Madero), Mildred Dunnock (Senora Espejo), Frank Silvera (General Huerta), Nina Varela (Aunt), Florenz Ames (Senor Espejo).

1953 Julius Caesar
Metro-Goldwyn-Mayer. Director: Joseph L. Mankiewicz. Producer: John Houseman. From the play by William Shakespeare. Music: Miklos Rozsa. Photographed by Joseph Ruttenberg. 121 minutes. New York premiere: June. With Marlon Brando (Mark Antony), James Mason (Brutus), John Gielgud (Cassius), Louis Calhern (Julius Caesar), Edmond O'Brien (Casca), Greer Garson (Calpurnia), Deborah Kerr (Portia), George Macready (Marullus), Michael Pate (Flavius), Alan Napier (Cicero), John Hoyt (Decius Brutus), Tom Powers (Metellus Cimber), Rhys Williams (Lucilius).

1953 The Wild One
Columbia. Director: Laslo Benedek. Producer: Stanley Kramer. Screenplay by John Paxton, based on a story by Frank Rooney. Music: Leith Stevens. Photographed by Hal Mohr. 79 minutes. New York premiere: December. With Marlon Brando (Johnnie), Mary Murphy (Kathie), Robert Keith (Harry Bleeker), Lee Marvin (Chino), Jay C. Flippen (Sheriff Singer), Peggy Maley (Mildred), Hugh Sanders (Charlie Thomas), Ray Teal (Frank Bleeker).

1954 On the Waterfront
Horizon–Columbia. Director: Elia Kazan. Producer: Sam Spiegel. Screenplay by Budd Schulberg, suggested by articles by Malcolm Johnson. Music: Leonard Bernstein. Photographed by Boris Kaufman. 107 minutes. New York premiere: July. With Marlon Brando (Terry Malloy), Eva Marie Saint (Edie Doyle), Karl Malden (Father Barry), Lee J. Cobb (Johnny Friendly), Rod Steiger (Charley Malloy), Pat Henning ('Kayo' Dugan), Leif Erickson (Glover), James Westerfield (Big Mac), John Heldabrand (Mutt), Rudy Bond (Moose), John Hamilton ('Pop' Doyle), Martin Balsam (Crime Commissioner), Pat Hingle (bartender).

1954 Désirée
20th Century-Fox. Director: Henry Koster. Producer: Julius Blaustein. Screenplay by Daniel Taradash, from the novel by Annemarie Selinko. Music: Alex North. Photographed by Milton Krasner. CinemaScope. De Luxe Colour. 110 minutes. New York premiere: November. With Marlon Brando (Napoleon), Jean Simmons (Désirée), Merle Oberon (Josephine), Michael Rennie (Bernadotte), Cameron Mitchell (Joseph Bonaparte), Elizabeth Sellars (Julie), Charlotte Austin (Paulette), Cathleen Nesbitt (Mme Bonaparte), Evelyn Varden (Marie), Isobel Elsom (Mme Clary), John Hoyt (Talleyrand), Alan Napier (Despreaux).

1955 **Guys and Dolls**
Samuel Goldwyn Productions–Metro-Goldwyn-Mayer. Director: Joseph L. Mankiewicz. Producer: Samuel Goldwyn. Screenplay by Mankiewicz, based on the play with book by Jo Swerling and Abe Burrows, adapted from a story by Damon Runyon. Music and lyrics: Frank Loesser. Photographed by Harry Stradling. CinemaScope. Eastman Colour. 149 minutes. New York premiere: November. With Marlon Brando (Sky Masterson), Jean Simmons (Sarah Brown), Frank Sinatra (Nathan Detroit), Vivian Blaine (Adelaide), Robert Keith (Lt Brannigan), Stubby Kaye (Nicely-Nicely Johnson), B. S. Silver (Big Jule), Johnny Silver (Benny Southstreet), Sheldon Leonard (Harry the Horse), Dan Dayton (Rusty Charlie), Regis Toomey (Arvid Abernathy).

1956 **The Teahouse of the August Moon**
Metro-Goldwyn-Mayer. Director: Daniel Mann. Producer: Jack Cummings. Screenplay by John Patrick, based on his play, adapted from the novel by Vern Sneider. Music: Saul Chaplin. Photographed by John Alton. CinemaScope. Metrocolor. 123 minutes. New York premiere: November. With Marlon Brando (Sakini), Glenn Ford (Captain Fisby), Machiko Kyo (Lotus Blossom), Eddie Albert (Captain McLean), Paul Ford (Colonel Purdy), Jun Negami (Mr Seiko), Nijiko Kiyokawa (Miss Higa Jiga).

1957 **Sayonara**
Goetz Pictures Inc.–Pennebaker Productions–Warner Bros. Director: Joshua Logan. Producer: William Goetz. Screenplay by Paul Osborn, from the novel by James A. Michener. Music: Franz Waxman. Photographed by Ellsworth Fredericks. Technirama. Technicolor. 147 minutes. New York premiere: December. With Marlon Brando (Major Lloyd Gruver), Miiko Taka (Hana-ogi), Red Buttons (Airman Joe Kelly), Patricia Owens (Eileen Webster), Ricardo Montalban (Nakamura), Myoshi Umeki (Katsumi), Kent Smith (General Webster), Martha Scott (Mrs Webster), James Garner (Captain Bailey), Doug Watson (Colonel Calhoun).

1958 **The Young Lions**
20th Century Fox. Director: Edward Dmytryk. Producer: Al Lichtman. Screenplay by Edward Anhalt, from the novel by Irwin Shaw. Music: Hugo Friedhofer. Photographed by Joe MacDonald. CinemaScope. 167 minutes. New York premiere: April. With Marlon Brando (Christian Diestl), Montgomery Clift (Noah Ackerman), Dean Martin (Michael Whiteacre), Hope Lange (Hope Plowman), Barbara Rush (Margaret Freemantle), May Britt (Gretchen Hardenberg), Maximilian Schell (Hardenberg), Dora Doll (Simone), Lee Van Cleef (Sgt Rickett), Liliane Montevecchi (Françoise), Arthur Franz (Lt Green).

1960 **The Fugitive Kind**
Jurow–Shepherd–Pennebaker–United Artists. Director: Sidney Lumet. Producers: Martin Jurow, Richard A. Shepherd. Screenplay by Tennessee Williams and Meade Roberts, from the play by Williams, *Orpheus Descending*. Music: Kenyon Hopkins. Photographed by Boris Kaufman. 121 minutes. New York premiere: April. With Marlon Brando (Val Xavier), Anna Magnani (Lady Torrance), Joanne Woodward (Carol Cutrere), Maureen Stapleton (Vee Talbot), Victor Jory (Jabe Torrance), R. G. Armstrong (Sheriff Talbot), Emory Richardson (Uncle Pleasant), Spivy (Ruby Lightfoot).

1961 **One-Eyed Jacks**
Pennebaker–Paramount. Director: Marlon Brando. Producer: Frank P. Rosenberg. Screenplay by Guy Trosper and Calder Willingham, based on the novel *The Authentic Death of Hendry Jones* by Charles Neider. Music: Hugo Friedhofer. Photographed by Charles Lang Jr. Vistavision. Technicolor. 141 minutes. New York premiere: March. With Marlon Brando (Rio), Karl Malden (Dad Longworth), Pina Pellicer (Louisa), Katy Jurado (Maria), Ben Johnson (Bob Amory), Slim Pickens (Lon), Larry Duran (Modesto), Sam Gilman (Harvey), Timothy Carey (Howard Tetley), Miriam Colon (Redhead), Elisha Cook (Bank Teller).

1962 **Mutiny on the Bounty**
Arcola–Metro-Goldwyn-Mayer. Director: Lewis Milestone. Producer: Aaron Rosenberg. Screenplay by Charles Lederer, based on the novel by Charles Nordhoff and James Norman Hall. Music: Bronislau Kaper. Photographed by Robert L. Surtees. Ultra Panavision 70. Technicolor. 185 minutes. New York premiere: November. With Marlon Brando (Fletcher Christian),

Trevor Howard (William Bligh), Richard Harris (John Mills), Hugh Griffith (Alexander Smith), Richard Haydn (William Brown), Tim Seely (Edward Young), Percy Herbert (Matthew Quintal), Gordon Jackson (Edward Birkett), Noel Purcell (William McCoy), Duncan Lamont (John Williams), Chips Rafferty (Michael Byrne), Ashley Cowan (Samuel Mack), Eddie Byrne (John Fryer), Frank Silvera (Minarii), Tarita (Maimiti).

1963 The Ugly American

Universal–International. Director and producer: George Englund. Screenplay by Stewart Stern, based on the novel by William J. Lederer and Eugene Burdick. Music: Frank Skinner. Photographed by Clifford Stine. Eastmancolor. 120 minutes. New York premiere: April. With Marlon Brando (Harrison Carter MacWhite), Eija Okada (Deong), Sandra Church (Marion MacWhite), Pat Hingle (Homer Atkins), Arthur Hill (Grainger), Jocelyn Brando (Emma Atkins).

1964 Bedtime Story

Lankershim–Pennebaker–Universal International. Director: Ralph Levy. Producer: Stanley Shapiro. Screenplay by Shapiro and Paul Henning. Music: Hans J. Salter. Photographed by Clifford Stine. Eastman Colour. 99 minutes. New York premiere: June. With Marlon Brando (Fred Benson), David Niven (Lawrence Jamison), Shirley Jones (Janet Walker), Dody Goodman (Fanny Eubank), Aram Stephan (Monsieur André), Parley Baer (Col Williams), Marie Windsor (Mrs Sutton), Rebecca Sand (Mrs Trumble).

1965 Morituri retitled The Saboteur, Code Name 'Morituri'

Arcola–Colony–20th Century-Fox. Director: Bernhard Wicki. Producer: Aaron Rosenberg. Screenplay by Daniel Taradash, based on the novel by Werner Jörg Lüdecke. Music: Jerry Goldsmith. Photographed by Conrad Hall. 122 minutes. New York premiere: August. With Marlon Brando (Robert Crain), Yul Brynner (Captain Müller), Trevor Howard (Colonel Statter), Janet Margolin (Esther), Martin Benrath (Kruse), Hans Christian Blech (Donkeyman), Wally Cox (Dr Ambach).

1966 The Chase

Horizon–Lone Star–Columbia. Director: Arthur Penn. Producer: Sam Spiegel. Screenplay by Lillian Hellman, based on the novel and play by Horton Foote. Music: John Barry. Photographed by Joseph LaShelle. Panavision. Technicolor. 133 minutes. New York premiere: February. With Marlon Brando (Calder), Jane Fonda (Anna Reeves), Robert Redford (Bubber Reeves), E. G. Marshall (Val Rogers), Angie Dickinson (Ruby Calder), Janice Rule (Emily Stewart), Miriam Hopkins (Mrs Reeves), Martha Hyer (Mary Fuller), Richard Bradford (Damon Fuller), Robert Duvall (Edwin Stewart), James Fox (Jake Rogers), Diana Hyland (Elizabeth Rogers), Henry Hull (Briggs), Jocelyn Brando (Mrs Briggs), Katherine Walsh (Verna Dee), Lori Martin (Cutie), Marc Seton (Paul), Joel Fluellen (Lester Johnson), Nydia Westman (Mrs Henderson), Bruce Cabot (Sol), Eduardo Ciannelli, Grady Sutton (Guests at party).

1966 The Appaloosa (in Great Britain: Southwest to Sonora)

Universal. Director: Sidney J. Furie. Producer: Alan Miller. Screenplay by James Bridges and Roland Kibbee, based on the novel by Robert MacLeod. Music: Frank Skinner. Photographed by Russell Metty. Techniscope. Technicolor. 98 minutes. New York premiere: September. With Marlon Brando (Matt), Anjanette Comer (Trini), John Saxon (Chuy), Rafael Campos (Paco), Miriam Colon (Ana), Emilio Fernandez (Lazaro), Alex Montoya (Squint-Eye), Frank Silvera (Ramos).

1967 A Countess from Hong Kong

British: Universal. Director: Charles Chaplin. Producer: Jerome Epstein. Screenplay by Chaplin. Music: Chaplin. Photographed by Arthur Ibbetson. Technicolor. 120 minutes. London premiere: January. With Marlon Brando (Ogden), Sophia Loren (Natascha), Sydney Chaplin (Harvey), Tippi Hedren (Martha), Patrick Cargill (Hudson), Michael Medwin (John Felix), Oliver Johnston (Clark), John Paul (Captain), Margaret Rutherford (Miss Gaulswallow), Angela Scoular (Society Girl), Charles Chaplin (an Old Steward).

1967 Reflections in a Golden Eye

Warner Bros: Seven Arts. Director: John Huston. Producer: Ray Stark. Screenplay by Chapman Mortimer and Gladys Hill, based on the novel by Carson McCullers. Music: Toshiro Mayuzumi. Photographed by Aldo Tonti. Panavision. Technicolor. 109 minutes. New York premiere: October. With Elizabeth Taylor (Leonora

Penderton), Marlon Brando (Major Weldon Penderton), Brian Keith (Lt-Col Morris Langdon), Julie Harris (Alison Langdon), Robert Forster (Private Williams), Zorro David (Anacleto), Gordon Mitchell (Stables Sergeant), Irvin Dugan (Captain Weincheck).

1968 **Candy**
American–French–Italian: Selmur Pictures (Hollywood)–Dear Film (Rome)–Corona (Paris). Distributed by Cinerama. Director: Christian Marquand. Producer: Robert Haggiag. Screenplay by Buck Henry, based on the novel by Terry Southern and Mason Hoffenberg. Music: Dave Grusin. Songs sung by The Byrds and Steppenwolf. Photographed by Giuseppe Rotunno. Technicolor. 124 minutes. New York premiere: December. With Ewa Aulin (Candy), Marlon Brando (Grindl), Richard Burton (McPhisto), James Coburn (Dr Krankheit), Walter Matthau (General Smight), Charles Aznavour (The Hunchback), John Huston (Dr Dunlap), John Astin (Daddy/Uncle Jack), Elsa Martinelli (Livia), Ringo Starr (Emmanuel), Enrico Maria Salerno (Jonathan J. John), Sugar Ray Robinson (Zero), Anita Pallenberg (Nurse Bullock), Lea Padovani (Silvia), Florinda Bolkan (Lolita), Marilù Tolo (Conchita), Nicoletta Machiavelli (Marquita), Umberto Orsini (1st Hood).

1969 **The Night of the Following Day**
Gina–Universal. Director and producer: Hubert Cornfield. Screenplay by Cornfield and Robert Phippeny, based on the novel *The Snatchers* by Lionel White. Music: Stanley Myers. Photographed by Willy Kurant. Technicolor. 93 minutes. New York premiere: January. With Marlon Brando (Bud), Richard Boone (Leer), Rita Moreno (Vi), Pamela Franklin (The Girl), Jess Hahn (Wally), Gérard Buhr (Gendarme).

1970 **Queimada!**
Italian–French: P.E.A. (Rome)–Les Productions Artistes Associés (Paris). Distributed by United Artists. Director: Gillo Pontecorvo. Producer: Alberto Grimaldi. Screenplay by Franco Solinas and Giorgio Arlorio, from a story by Pontecorvo, Solinas and Arlorio. Music: Ennio Morricone. Photographed by Marcello Gatti and Giuseppe Bruzzolini. De Luxe Color. 132 minutes (112 minutes in the U.S.A. and Britain). Italian premiere: January. New York premiere:

October. With Marlon Brando (Sir William Walker), Evaristo Marquez (José Dolores), Renato Salvatore (Teddy Sanchez), Norman Hill (Shelton), Tom Lyons (General Prada).

1971 **The Nightcomers**
Scimitar–Avco Embassy. An Elliott Kastner–Jay Kanter–Alan Ladd Jr Production. Director and producer: Michael Winner. Screenplay by Michael Hastings, based on characters created by Henry James. Music: Jerry Fielding. Photographed by Robert Paynter. Technicolor. 96 minutes. New York premiere: December. London premiere: May 1972. With Marlon Brando (Peter Quint), Stephanie Beacham (Miss Jessel), Thora Hird (Mrs Grose), Harry Andrews (Master of the House), Verna Harvey (Flora), Christopher Ellis (Miles), Anna Palk (New Governess).

1972 **The Godfather**
Alfran Productions–Paramount. Director: Francis Ford Coppola. Producer: Albert S. Ruddy. Screenplay by Mario Puzo and Coppola, based on the novel by Puzo. Music: Nino Rota. Photographed by Gordon Willis. Technicolor. 175 minutes. New York premiere: March. With Marlon Brando (Don Vito Corleone), Al Pacino (Michael Corleone), James Caan (Sonny Corleone), Richard Castellano (Clemenza), Robert Duvall (Tom Hagan), Sterling Hayden (McCluskey), John Marley (Jack Woltz), Richard Conte (Barzini), Diane Keaton (Kay Adams), Al Lettieri (Sollozzo), Abe Vigoda (Tessio), Talia Shire (Connie Rizzi), Gianni Russo (Carlo Rizzi), John Cazale (Fredo Corleone), Rudy Bond (Cuneo), Al Martino (Johnny Fontane), Morgana King (Mama Corleone).

1972 **L'Ultimo Tango in Parigi/ Dernier Tango à Paris/ Last Tango in Paris**
Italian–French: P.E.A. Cinematografica (Rome)–Les Artistes Associés (Paris). Distributed by United Artists. Director: Bernardo Bertolucci. Producer: Alberto Grimaldi. Screenplay by Bertolucci and Franco Arcalli. Music: Gato Barbieri. Photographed by Vittorio Storaro. Technicolor. 129 minutes. New York premiere: October. Italian and French premieres: January 1973. With Marlon Brando (Paul), Maria Schneider (Jeanne), Jean-Pierre Léaud (Tom), Massimo Girotti (Marcel), Catherine Allégret (Catherine), Maria Michi (Rosa's mother).

Index

Page references in italics indicate illustrations

Acknowledgements

Our thanks to the following for permission to reproduce photographs: Culver Pictures Inc., Photoservice, Radio Times Hulton Picture Library (the real Zapata), United Artists, Warner Bros, 20th Century-Fox, Metro-Goldwyn-Mayer (CIC), Columbia, Paramount (CIC), Universal (CIC), Cinerama Releasing and Avco-Embassy; and to their representatives in their London distribution offices for their kindness and cooperation, and to the staff of the National Film Archive Stills Department, and the Cinema Bookshop.

Among the books consulted by the author are his own *The Great Movie Stars: The International Years*, and the following: *The Lonely Life* by Bette Davis; *Actors Talk About Acting* edited by Funke and Booth; *Broadway* by Brooks Atkinson; *Letters from an Actor* by William Redfield; *The Celluloid Muse* edited by Higham and Greenberg; *The Player* edited by Lillian and Helen Ross; *Who Killed Marilyn Monroe?* by Charles Hamblett and *The Dreams and the Dreamers* by Hollis Alpert. And the following newspapers and magazines: *Films Illustrated*, *The New York Times*, *Time Magazine*, *Esquire*, *Sight & Sound*, *The New York Herald-Tribune*, *Movie*, *Theatre Arts Monthly*, *The Sunday Times*, *Photoplay*, *Variety*, *The Observer*, *Show Magazine*, *Films and Filming*, *The New Statesman* and *Ciné-Revue*.